Natural
Care

TAKING CARE OF YOURSELF THE NATURAL WAY

Wendyl Nissen

Natural Care

Photography by Jane Ussher

ALLEN&UNWIN
SYDNEY · MELBOURNE · AUCKLAND · LONDON

To my dad, Cedric Nissen,
who has cared for me always

Contents

Introduction

I came up with the idea for this book during our first Covid-19 lockdown, in March 2020. I was in the middle of finishing my last book and had just lost all my magazine-writing work because Bauer, the publishing house that published most of our magazines, closed down. Bang, just like that.

My husband, Paul, who is also a freelance writer and lost his magazine and newspaper work as well, sat down with me and we worked out that if we both came up with a few book ideas we could at least earn some money from those as there would be no work coming from magazines.

This is the email I sent to Jenny Hellen, my publisher:

Mōrena,

So I've come up with an idea which I think works well especially in post-Covid times when people will need to provide more care for loved ones than they are used to. I also think that we are all going to realise that being in a good position health- and kindness-wise prepares us best for any dramas on the world stage. It will also fit into a new comfort category I am predicting.

This is such a 'me' email because I'm always predicting stuff — most of it incorrectly, much to my family's amusement. I'm always starting sentences with the words 'I reckon that . . .'

My family and friends always listen politely and nod. They know that it probably won't turn out that way but it's easier just to go along with it. (I get the same reaction when I tell them about my amazing nightly dreams, which I insist are messages and have meaning rather than just being the result of my brain doing some processing.)

I wrote that email on 20 April 2020, and at the time it was all a bit scary as we tried to work out how to live in a Covid world and eventually understand that what used to be normal never would be again.

As I write this, nearly 18 months after sending that email, I realise that the caring bit has eventuated. I think that most of us have reached out and supported more people than we would have before Covid, and that caring and checking in on others is now part of our daily lives. We have supported others through Covid whether it was driving an elderly neighbour to get her vaccine, supporting someone who lost work, or helping someone with a mental-health issue. We have all done this and we will continue to do this. Caring is the new normal.

But what I didn't predict is that we would end up with this feeling of isolation that we now have in New Zealand. We have lived a relatively free life, unheard of outside our borders, as month by month we have watched the rest of the world try and fail to contain Covid. We've had a few lockdowns but mostly we've enjoyed concerts, restaurants, parties, domestic holidays and working from home if we want to but don't really need to.

We read with pride and trepidation newspaper stories from overseas naming our country as the most preferred place to live and wonder what that means going forward. Will we be inundated with capitalist multi-billionaires paying $10 million for residency and buying up our land? Or will it mean we get to help more refugees from around the world who have nowhere to live?

So while we are caring, I think we are also getting used to the feeling of being part of the privileged few who live relatively free of Covid, at least at the time of writing. And that, I think, makes us turn inward.

I've spent more time in the past year looking at myself and my life than at any other time in my 59 years. I've gone from being someone who strides through life experiencing it as it happens, to doing what I do now — planning, learning, concentrating on what I can do with my life to give it meaning and keep safe. I feel like I've enrolled myself in a course called 'Post Covid Survival 101'.

I try not to think too much about what's going on outside of my country, because I can't work it out and neither can they.

So I turn to my garden, my animals, my books, my loved ones and I make sure I'm doing the best I can for them, which is much more than I used to do. But mostly I've turned to myself and learned how to do the best for me, physically and mentally. For the first time ever, I asked myself 'Am I the best I can be at the moment?', and my answer was no. I wasn't as healthy as I could be, I wasn't as stable mentally as I could be, and that concerned me. I found myself no longer happy to leave it up to chance. Chance had happened and its name was Covid-19.

This book is called *Natural Care* but it could also have been titled *How One Woman Pulled Her Britches Up and Got Real About Things*.

I feel safer living this life of inward thinking and changing my life from something a bit haphazard towards something that is planned and well thought out.

None of us know what's to come in this world, but at the moment we are the lucky five million who feel isolated but safer than most.

I read more books than I care to remember during this year of pulling my britches up and I learned more than I thought possible. I put so many new things into practice, things I should have done years ago.

Natural Care is a summary of that year and everything I learned. As I finished this book I knew that within these pages were some answers to questions I'm sure you've asked yourself as well. I hope you can find the will to pull your britches up too.

Self-care

Suddenly it's all about self. Self-care, self-love, self-awareness, self-healing, self-esteem, self-worth, self-definition.

Which is lovely in some ways. Your self is the type of person you are, especially the way you normally behave, look or feel, according to the *Oxford English Dictionary*.

So being yourself, and looking after yourself, is a good thing.

But as I was thinking about writing this chapter I walked past The Body Shop in a mall and saw the words 'Rise Up With Self-Love' plastered all over the back wall in huge type and I felt a bit nauseous.

My self is not some tool to be used by multinational corporates to market their products, I thought to myself. My self is mine. It is unique and special and identifies who I am. So fuck off, The Body Shop.

I did not go into The Body Shop and buy a pot of cream for my face because I rose up with my self-love.

Like so many things, it can be very hard to distinguish whether something is good for your wellbeing from the way it is presented to you through Instagram or other social media channels and marketing.

Mindfulness is something I believe big companies adopt along with the bowl of fruit in the cafeteria. The message is — we have given you a mindfulness course and we have given you a free banana, so if you're feeling tired and not spending enough time with your family and friends who nourish you because we made you work overtime and all through the weekend, then it's your fault. You just didn't do enough mindfulness practice or eat enough free fruit.

So let's explore self-care and what it should mean.

First you need to identify your self. For many women this is quite hard to do because as mothers, partners, sisters, grandmothers and workers we are often so busy taking care of everyone else's self that ours gets pushed far, far into the background.

I did this for many years when I was a full-time working mum of five children with a mortgage to pay. I was also a boss, which meant I cared for, or tried to care for, up to 30 staff. At that time it seemed incredibly selfish to stop in the middle of all that caring and put myself first.

Labour MP Kiri Allen talked very openly about this when she announced her diagnosis of stage three cervical cancer in April 2021. In her amazing Facebook post, which I encourage you to read if you haven't already, she said:

'Time passes. Work piles on. Going to the doctor for anything other than an emergency goes way down the priority list.

'In hindsight, there were lots of opportunities to go touch base with a doctor. But I didn't. I put it down to work, and was on the go, and "that stuff usually sorts itself out".'

Most of us will admit that we've done that. If it's not something that basically stops us from moving, we don't get it seen to straight away.

Kiri's openness about her diagnosis and her plea to other women to get a smear had a huge impact on so many women in Aotearoa.

'I've told a few folks by now, and often the question is, "Is there anything I can do?". My answer now is yes. Please, please, please — encourage your sisters, your mothers, your daughters, your friends — please #SmearYourMea — it may save your life — and we need you right here.'

I remember moaning to a friend about having to have a smear because I really, really dislike them and tense up and that makes it worse and then I cry or scream depending on my stress levels that day. My friend, quite rightly, said 'Well, how will you feel when you haven't prevented a completely preventable disease?' and so I went and had it and tensed up and cried. In my defence there are some quite good statistics that show I'm not alone in this. Bring on the self-smear kits.

Some of us, having spent so long without a sense of self, can find it difficult to get in touch. Where is she? How do I know what she's like? Will I even like her?

Of course you will like her, but she might not be much like who you are right now. That is the lesson I had to learn. In the early 2000s, when I started trying to find out who I really was, it was a long process that began by getting rid of everyone who was defining who I was at the time. I had bosses, parents, siblings, friends, a husband and children, who all reflected back to me who I was to them. My bosses wanted me to be successful for them, to be a bit of a tough bitch, to work long hours and make them lots of money.

My parents, well that's a whole other story I wrote about in my last book, but I was painted by my mother as a difficult slut who embarrassed her and should be ridiculed at every opportunity. I'm shocked to say that I believed her for a long time.

I had a difficult relationship with my brother, which is all I'll say about that. And then I had my friends, some who wanted me to be the same person my bosses wanted but funnier. I no longer have those friends. The others liked me the way I was with all my ups and downs, and I felt I could be honest with them and have bad days and really enjoyable good days.

My husband and my children, well they were the ones who reflected my true self.

In them I saw that I was kind and caring, nice to be around, strong and reliant when I needed to be and soft and cuddly too. I also saw that no matter who I wanted to be or what I wanted to be, my husband and children were my greatest supporters. Unlike my bosses and some friends, they were happy for me to change — quite a lot.

I decided to spend more time with my family and friends and see what happened. I gave up full-time work and went freelance when my youngest daughter Pearl started school in 2003, and that's when I found myself in my kitchen making soap and bread from scratch, roasting coffee beans on my stove, and reading books on gardening, nutrition and the environment.

Slowly and surely I began to glimpse my self again.

One day I was digging in the garden, which back then was an activity I was just rediscovering, and I had a flashback to when I was 20, living in a flat in Bond Street, Grey Lynn. I remembered digging up the garden where I had planted carrots and lettuce and other veges and triumphantly taking them as a salad to a party, much to the distress of my friends, who thought I had lost my mind.

When I baked a loaf of bread, I remembered being 18 and living in another flat in Freemans Bay, and making my first loaf of wholemeal bread. It was a disaster that looked, felt and tasted like a brick, but I loved making it.

I still have the cookbook responsible for that brick of bread. It is called *Conscious Cookery: Vegetarian cookery without the use of meat, fish, fowl and eggs* and promotes vegetarianism, total abstinence from alcohol and drugs, moral living and daily meditation.

I remember sprouting beansprouts and cooking things like lentil pie — something I now do again.

When I was in the middle of reading one of many scientific books as research for this book, I realised that I used to love science. As a child I adored my chemistry set, setting myself up in the laundry to make various potions. I had a darkroom in the basement where I developed photos in three trays of chemicals. In high school I studied the sciences and got good marks for chemistry, biology and physics in School Certificate. I wanted to be a scientist, but somehow deviated from that course and headed towards journalism.

In my forties I started experimenting and creating a whole range of natural cleaning products out of stuff I developed in my kitchen. I recently visited the Green Goddess business I started (it now has new owners) and looked at the dozens of products proudly sitting on the shelves. I was reminded that I had created each and every one of them from scratch, using science and some really old domestic housewifery books. So my real self loves science.

I realised as I discovered my self that she had been there in the early days as I headed into adulthood and had somehow been pushed to the back as more important things came along, like a career and family.

Sometimes I like to think about the self I have now and compare it with the self I had at 18. There are many similarities. Both of us really love swimming in the ocean, we love growing and eating good food, we like to sew, we love animals, we love reading, we love writing.

The only difference is that my old self drank and took some drugs while my new self does very little of that nonsense. My old self didn't like children very much and my new self loves them, obviously. And my old self lived in a bikini and lay in the sun a lot while my new self does none of that and frequently has early melanoma moles cut out.

Some people advise getting in touch with your self by putting pictures up on the wall of you at a younger age, but I don't advise that. How you look — mainly younger and thinner — has no bearing on who your self is.

You'll know when you've found your self because you will start to feel authentic. You will feel that every time you do something, it's because you want to do it, you feel good doing it and you feel better for having done it.

It's a hard feeling to describe but you'll know it when you feel it. It might be that you become happier all round, or you just feel warmer or more in touch, or you finally feel like you.

I recently described it to Paul as I was considering whether to take up a new job opportunity.

'I think it should feel like fairy dust is falling on me, and this one doesn't. In my gut it feels wrong. So no fairy dust, no me.'

Parenting yourself

I hesitated to include a section on parenting yourself in this book. The whole issue of childhood trauma staying with us into adulthood and the need to rid ourselves of that trauma and re-parent ourselves is a big topic. There are many books written about it in great detail. When I read

How to Do the Work by Dr Nicole LePera, who has a huge social media following, I realised about halfway through that it was triggering me. This means that it reminded me of stuff that went on in my childhood with my mother. I suddenly felt really ill because my trauma and stress always goes to my stomach. I put the book down and the next day gingerly picked it up again to see if I was just imagining the whole triggering thing, but no, here it came again.

Here's the thing. If you had a difficult childhood and you were parented in a traumatic way, there is no doubt you have been affected by it. But some people cope with it and get on with their lives. My mother was cruel and difficult and sometimes wouldn't talk to me for days. She had three different personalities and body-shamed me all through my life — I wrote all about that in my book *My Mother and Other Secrets*. My mother didn't tell me she loved me or was proud of me until her last years, when dementia took away all her memories of her own cruel childhood and allowed her the freedom to be who she was meant to be. A loving, kind, thoughtful mother not plagued by mental demons.

I've done some work on this but certainly not the peel-away-the-onion-skin-down-to-the-very-core-type work and that is fine with me. For some people that kind of work really helps. It's really up to you what you do about that.

But one very helpful thing I did discover is to sort of parent myself.

If I'm upset or stressed I will take a moment, put my hand on my heart and say to myself 'Are you okay, darling? What do you need?' as I would to any of my children if they were upset. My child would then tell me what was going on and we would work together to see what we could do about that and my child would feel better. So I do that for myself.

As an example, I often feel stressed and anxious and have no idea why. Taking a moment to sit with my hand on my heart will usually deliver the reason to me. Perhaps I had some terse words with my husband, or work wasn't going well or a friend had annoyed me. I identify the reason behind the feeling, and then my self-parent and I work out what to do about it.

Before I know it I'm feeling better and I have a plan. I am a good mother, something I've worked really hard to be, so now I too get the benefit of the mothering that I never got as a child.

Another thing I do before I go to bed is sit on the side of my bed and tell myself that I am safe and well. I go over all the good things that have happened in my day. Some people keep a gratitude diary, I just say them in my head.

When I started doing this Paul would walk in and give me a funny look. In the 26 years we've been together, I had never before sat on the side of the bed and looked thoughtful.

'Are you okay? You look weird,' he'd say.

'I'm just taking a moment,' I'd reply.

Now he doesn't say anything and gets on with getting ready for bed, which usually involves making sure the bed is tucked in tight, pillows are beaten to within an inch of their life and pyjamas are put on and buttoned. I used to find this quite distracting as I was having my thoughtful time, but now I just tune it out.

Gratitude — the act of expressing appreciation for things in your life — has become a 'healthy mind' thing to do. Study after study has found a robust association between high levels of gratitude and wellbeing, including protection from stress and depression, more fulfilling relationships, better sleep and greater resilience.

But some of us need to practise it. You might have skipped past the fact that the woman behind you at the coffee shop picked up your dropped bus card, or a complete stranger smiled at you on the street. These are nice things to feel grateful for, but sometimes in our busy lives

we just feel and release our gratitude instead of revisiting it later and getting the wonderful warmth all over again. It definitely takes practice — after a while you will find yourself noting something during the day to remember that evening during your thoughtful session.

My mother never complimented me or told me I was beautiful. If someone told me I was pretty, she would immediately put me down so that I 'wouldn't get too up myself'. So when I grew up, if someone told me this (often several times a day in the case of my husband), I wouldn't hear it. I didn't know how to accept those words because I hadn't had any practice. I didn't know what to do. For years Paul would notice that if he said 'You look beautiful today' I would get a far-away look and do my best to run out of the room.

Now if someone compliments me, I hear their words, and feel them, and love it, and then I feel them all over again when I'm having my bedtime thoughtful session. One day perhaps I'll even believe them.

Letting the difficult back in

As women, we learn to filter ourselves when answering questions because we want to keep everyone calm and happy. That's our job.

Imagine your partner coming into the room and saying 'How are you?'

Now imagine you replied with an honest, authentic appraisal of your life that day, that went something like 'I am completely stuffed because I've spent all day running around looking after people at work, and then picking up the kids and cooking them dinner, and I've got the worst period, which is giving me horrible cramps, and a pimple the size of a walnut on my forehead, well at least it feels that way, and I'm really pissed off you left for work and didn't stack the dishwasher or put it on, and I've just done another load of washing, which I will hang out after dinner because I won't have time in the morning. Oh and your mother called.'

Instead we usually say 'Oh I'm okay, bit busy but . . . you know.'

We do this because if we said what was really going on, we'd be called 'difficult'.

I so hate that word and despise anyone who uses it in front of the word 'woman'.

In my life I have often been called a 'difficult woman' simply because I do not apply a filter and I say the truth. I recently interviewed another woman who is often called difficult, Dr Siouxsie Wiles, the microbiologist who helped us all understand the science behind the Covid-19 pandemic. She helped us feel safe and calm, which doesn't sound like a difficult woman to me.

She told me that she knows some people describe her as a 'difficult woman' but she doesn't care.

'A lot of my collaborations haven't worked out because I have clear ideas about how I want science to be done. I'm quite demanding in that I want us to do it well, use our resources well and communicate that research beyond other academics. We have an obligation to communicate our work to other people. So yes, maybe I'm seen as difficult but maybe the system is the problem and it struggles with people like me who think the system is wrong and should be changed.'

Siouxsie keeps her social media accounts active despite being viciously trolled, because she reasons she can take it and if she shut them down those trolls would just pick on someone else.

When you parent yourself you are allowed to say difficult things and you will be heard, possibly for the first time in your life. Here is my guide to having a parenting session with yourself.

1. Sit alone in a quiet place — like you're going to meditate.

2. Place your hand over your heart, or anywhere else that feels comfortable.

3. Ask yourself 'What do I need?'

4. Answer yourself honestly. 'I need a hug, I need a nap, I need to be able to not care about such-and-such or so-and-so, and I need a chocolate,' might be your answer.

5. Then act as you would if you were a good mother, and help yourself get those things. Become your best advocate and carer.

Since I learned how to do this, I check in with myself most days, especially if I'm feeling 'off'. This practice usually uncovers why I'm feeling out of sorts, and how I can best help myself. Anyone can take a nap, but not everyone has their own parent making sure it happens because we don't want you getting grouchy. (Using baby talk does sometimes help, by the way.)

One thing to be aware of with this practice is that when you are parenting yourself, you may need others to help you. You can give yourself a hug but they are much better coming from someone you love.

Often being able to not care about a problem involves talking it out with someone, such as a partner, friend or counsellor. However, those people might have a different opinion about what you should do. Don't listen to them. You are in an intimate, authentic, truthful relationship with yourself and only you know what you need. You're not co-parenting here.

Getting help

Sometimes parenting yourself is not enough. You are aware who you are, you are listening to what you need, but you don't have the tools in the toolbox to fix it. That is when you might like to get a therapist.

A year after Covid arrived, I started noticing a lot of articles in the media about mental health. Covid is not good for people who are struggling with mental-health issues, but the silver lining is that we are now talking about mental health more than any other generation.

No one really knows what goes on in our brains. But we do know that our brain controls everything our body does and it also controls whether we are happy or sad, depressed or manic. Some people wake up quite happy most days, like my husband. Others wake up barely able to find the will to live. Why do some people struggle with anxiety and depression while others seem to waltz through life with no issues whatsoever?

We don't really know yet, but more and more studies are focusing on our brains, looking at genetics, nutrition, LSD treatments and many, many other ways to try to help those who struggle.

What we do know is that our brain is unique to who we are. As Bill Bryson says in his book *The Body: A guide for occupants*, 'Your brain is you. Everything else is just plumbing and scaffolding.'

Our brain manages our breathing, digestion and body temperature. It manages our movement, balance and speech. It manages our thinking, emotions, behaviour and senses.

It is also the keeper of our memories, the creator of our dreams, the definer of our unique personality.

It can also send us into a pit of despair, freeze us to the ground with anxiety and stop us sleeping.

For something with all that power, you'd think we might spend a bit

more time caring for it. But like so many things, that is just not something we've been taught how to do. For many years we have disassociated from our brain, relying on it to keep on working despite abuse from alcohol, drugs, not eating properly or a good knocking around on the rugby field.

Next time you are thinking about why you should eat well, sleep well and exercise, include your brain in the conversation, not just the size of your waist or your biceps.

OVER THE YEARS, Big Food (that's the large industrial food producers and manufacturers) have tried to persuade us that certain foods are good for our brains. For example, I grew up watching commercials telling us that fish was essential for a healthy brain. I think it probably is, in as much as eating a wide range of foods is good for us. But what our brain basically needs is a good healthy diet full of whole foods, and as few processed foods as possible. And iron. It needs iron, so make sure you eat foods rich in that one. And water. Staying hydrated helps your brain work, too.

Your brain is made up mainly of water, fat and protein, and uses up to 400 calories a day. Start thinking of it as a living thing that needs good nutrition to give you the best results. The better the nutrition you give your brain, the better and harder it will work for you.

Boundary setting

Part of looking after yourself is setting boundaries. Boundary setting is yet another thing we've been taught not to do. We are not allowed to simply say 'No, I don't want to come to your party because I don't feel like it.' Instead we have to make up a lie, which makes us feel bad, or just not turn up and then lie about having a sick child or a flat car battery.

We are also supposed to let people hurt us because they are part of our family. Family first. We are also supposed to let friends hurt us because friendships matter and you don't break up with friends. We are also supposed to let our children hurt us. We are also supposed to let our bosses hurt us.

What would it feel like if we set some boundaries so that the number of times we experience hurt is vastly reduced?

Since I found my self I have worked really hard to protect her. I set boundaries and hold them firmly. I have lost friends. I didn't see some members of my family for years. I went out less to social functions I knew I wouldn't enjoy. I resigned from jobs with unsupportive bosses. I created checklists that I consult before saying 'yes' to anything, whether it be a new job, a speaking gig, a friendship or a social occasion.

Here's one of my checklists, in case it's of use to you too.

Thinking about the decision in front of you:

1. Will you just want to curl up under the duvet rather than attend this event when the time comes? Be honest.

2. Will this take you away from stuff you would rather be doing, even if that is just lying on the couch reading a book?

3. Are you agreeing to do this because you feel you should, i.e. supporting someone or something you don't really have a connection to, or do you feel genuinely uplifted about supporting this person or thing? If you don't, don't do it.

4. Will you have to give up something you were really looking forward to, like having the grandkids to stay, in order to attend this event? If so, don't do it.

5. When you imagine a world without this (job, friend, commitment) in it, how does that look? If it looks bloody great, then resign, distance or refuse.

6. Every time you think of this thing, does your stomach churn and do you pull a face? Don't do it.

P.S. It's okay to change your mind and ring up and cancel once you've thought about it and realised it's a bad idea. A week's notice is polite.

And you know what? I feel free, because boundaries work. Remember that when you set a boundary, you are the only person you have to convince. It doesn't matter how other people react to that boundary. It is your job to hold and enforce it for yourself.

I recently set a boundary around a job I was leaving. I had been uncomfortable in this workplace for some time and had reached the stage where I seriously didn't want anything to do with what was going on there. Well before my last day I clearly said that I would just like to finish up, get in my car and drive north from Auckland to my home. No fuss. Please respect this.

I knew my boundary wouldn't be respected. I knew there would be a need in this dysfunctional environment to pretend that all was well and to spray the workplace with a fog of fantasy good vibes.

When I arrived at work I left my handbag in the car, so that when I left the office it wouldn't be obvious I was leaving for good. I pocketed my phone and keys in my jeans and that was all I carried into the building.

I finished up and hugged a couple of my adorable co-workers, who were well aware of my boundary. But as I was getting into my car I was instructed to get back inside for a presentation of flowers and a gift and a speech.

Once upon a time I would have gone back in because I wouldn't have wanted to be rude. But I felt that it was also rude to not respect my boundary, especially when I had asked for it in advance and been very clear about it. My boundary had been ignored because a fog of fantasy good vibes was more important than respecting me. I knew that if I had to stand there and listen to lies I would open my mouth and be honest and wouldn't stop for a long, long time! I'm a truth teller, which sometimes gets me in a lot of trouble. So I stuck to my guns, some flowers were hastily brought out and given to me as I got in the car and I was told rather grumpily that my leaving gift would be sent to me.

It never was. Which just goes to show how much that gift really meant. It was simply a prop for show.

That's okay. I wasn't cut out to stand uncomfortably in a room of people and play the part of someone who was sad to leave, while other people played the part of wonderful, caring individuals when they had been anything but.

Difficult woman? Absolutely.

Nature

As I was about to write this piece on nature and mental health, it was a dark, rainy afternoon and I was feeling a bit grumpy. I left my lovely, warm house with its lovely, warm fire, put on my raincoat and headed out

into the pouring rain to walk my dogs. I never can resist that gorgeous look dogs give you when it is time to give them some exercise.

I had just had a disagreement with my 89-year-old father, who lives with us, and knew that some time in nature would get rid of the ill feeling. My father and I don't actually fight, but he is an old white man who has spent 89 years being listened to and taken seriously, as was the custom, and now he feels he knows better. This is not unusual behaviour for old white men. So we often have these 'exchanges' where he drives me nuts and I drive him nuts because unlike everyone everywhere else in his life I don't always agree with old white men!

I was also a bit lonely as Paul had been working in Auckland for a few nights and my self was unsettled.

I took the dogs and headed into the rain down the paddock to the beach. When I hit the sand, the sun shone through and there was the most beautiful rainbow. Just for me. Some would say this was some divine intervention, but I knew it was just nature. And only nature interrupts a rainstorm with a rainbow. The dogs and I walked towards it and had a much longer walk than I had intended.

As I headed back up the paddock, feeling much better, Paul yelled out from the veranda, having arrived home early. My world was back to normal.

By the way, my father wouldn't have been at all upset. He would have poured himself an evening glass of wine and said to himself 'She always was a bit difficult', parroting exactly what my mother said about me all my life.

Just google 'nature' and 'mental health' and you'll find many studies that prove that being in nature is good for your mind. The most recent study I could find recommended just two hours in nature per week to boost health and wellbeing. It's beneficial even if you just sit in it — you don't have to join a tramping club or even walk a lot. Just go outside for a while and see what happens. In this country we are so lucky to be near the bush or a beach pretty much wherever we live. So find some bush or beach and give yourself a 30-minute walk.

I once interviewed Green Party co-leader Marama Davidson for the *New Zealand Woman's Weekly* and I asked what brings her joy. She told me that getting out in her local park was the key.

'I know that my mental health relies on me touching nature, which sounds so clichéd but it's so true. I live near Tōtara Park in Manurewa, which is home to a massive stand of tōtara trees and rivers and creeks. To get out of the house and go for a walk in the bush brings me joy. Anything with bush or sea, and up in the Hokianga. That place literally represents my mecca of joy. I live in a busy suburb right on a main road so when I go up there I can't hear anything. There are birds and no traffic and no tooting horns and just the ocean down below.

'I don't think I get nearly enough joy as I would like. I have learned in this role to be proactive. I can't just think it's going to happen naturally. I have to make space.'

Tōtara Park is a 216-hectare reserve in South Auckland that provides its residents with bush walks, mountain-biking trails and natural spaces in which to commune with nature. There are many parks just like this all over New Zealand, which are free to use for all of us.

I could say be mindful and breathe, but actually just get out there and do it. Resist the urge to put earbuds in your ears and block off the sounds of nature, and resist the urge to take a friend with you.

Go alone and turn on all your senses. Consciously say to yourself that you are going to hear, watch and smell everything.

Your first time won't have a huge effect on you but I guarantee you will feel better. The next time you will notice a flower or a plant growing on the side of the path and stop to look at it. The next time you will hear birdsong and stop to see if you can spot the bird making it. The next

time you'll look forward to hearing that bird or seeing the plant again. And there you go — you are using nature for the purpose that it was quite possibly intended. To make us feel alive.

Those of us who have children will remember that taking them on a simple walk outside when they were little was a long and involved affair, because it's instinctive for children to notice nature. They stop and look at everything, picking, smelling, noticing a simple daisy on the way to school. And how many times did we say 'Hurry up or we'll be late!' instead of just going with it and apologising to the teacher when we delivered our nature-infused child to the classroom?

When I'm working I will take a break three or four times a day to go outside, no matter what the weather's doing. Usually I have jobs to do, like feeding the hens or planting some veggies, and other times I will find I start doing something unplanned like pruning the roses or sitting with the hens and just being. Then after about 20 minutes I get up and go back inside and pick up where I left off writing, feeling like I've just had two cigarettes and a cup of coffee in the old days when I was a journalist at *The Auckland Star*. That's what everyone did for a break from writing back then, inside at our desks. A great cloud of smoke always hung over the newsroom on deadline.

Sometimes if I'm tired or feeling anxious, I will lie down on the grass in the sun. I don't think I'd feel comfortable doing that in the city, but maybe we should? Maybe the sight of someone lying down on the grass in the sun doing nothing should be seen as a good thing, where we think, Oh well done, that woman is really looking after herself, instead of wondering if she's okay or unconscious.

The wonderful thing about nature as therapy is that it's free and it's right there all the time, day or night, ready to be of service. The only equipment you need is some wet-weather gear so that you can get out there even in a storm, which is quite empowering. I do it often.

I've also read some recent research that suggests that being around water or 'blue space' may be just as restorative as spending time in 'green space' such as bush and parks.

And another survey, this time studying 18,000 people in 18 countries, found that spending time in and around the coast, rivers, lakes and even fountains boosted mental and physical wellbeing.

This is hardly surprising, as we all know how glorious we feel after a day at the beach. I used to put that down to the immense amount of sunshine but now that I protect myself from the sun, I still get a sun-kissed feeling of pure relaxation and collapse into bed feeling fully rested and amazing. Nature works her magic again.

Surge capacity

One thing we are probably all dealing with in these Covid times is surge capacity. It's something that kicks in during stressful times that enables us to cope with disasters like earthquakes or floods. Our capacity surges, we deal with it, then we return to normal. But with Covid nothing is quite normal any more and possibly never will be again in the way we've thought of 'normal' in the past.

Science defines surge capacity as a system of biological and psychological adaptations that help us get through difficult times. It's similar to the burst of adrenaline people get when in a life-or-death situation where they have to act.

We can deal with any number of hardships, whether it's physical hardship like limited food or dealing with the elements, during or just after a natural disaster, or an emotional hardship such as dealing with a romantic break-up or a major project at work that's taken over our lives. But we can't stretch our own internal resources indefinitely to deal with those situations. Eventually, we need a break. And when no break is in sight, we crash.

I interviewed US science journalist Tara Haelle, who wrote a compelling piece about how her 'surge capacity' had run out and what she did to create her new normal.

She told me that the problem is that surge capacity doesn't stretch out indefinitely, yet the pandemic is going on and on. And dealing with it requires energy that you don't realise you're using.

'You're just trying to survive and keep all the balls in the air, and it's not until you start dropping one ball after another and realising you can't pick them all back up that it hits you how bone-tired you are.'

We talked about the necessity of self-care in these times and she pointed out that her self-care used to involve getting a massage, going out for coffee, or going to a bar with her husband. All these activities were off the table when Covid arrived.

So she interviewed surgeon and author of *The Resilience Bank Account*, Dr Michael Maddaus, who recommended that people with depleted surge capacity find a kind of 'creation' activity that involves both a planning element and an in-the-now moment.

'Some neurotransmitters in our brains fire off when we're planning something, generating the feeling of excitement we feel while planning. And other neurotransmitters thrill at an experience itself while we're in the moment. That's why artistic pursuits are especially important — when you plan a painting and then get lost in the act of painting, heading toward the goal of a finished product, you're activating both types of transmitters at the same time. But it doesn't need to be painting, or even art. It can be cooking, gardening, home improvements, playing a game with your family, photographing nature, or any number of other activities. If there was ever a time for us to appreciate the necessity of the arts and leisure in our lives, it's now.'

Finally, Tara said Dr Maddaus introduced her to the idea of a resilience bank account, the act of intentionally incorporating various coping tools into your daily life before you need them to help you deal with adversity later.

'Even though we're already in the midst of it, we can still begin trying to work on the elements he lists in particular: sleep, nutrition, exercise, meditation, self-compassion, gratitude, connection, and saying no, which I also interpret as allowing yourself to sometimes sit and "do nothing".'

Anxiety

A big part of self-care is finding a way to get through anxiety. If you don't suffer from anxiety, then you are a very lucky person. Our health statistics tell us that one in four New Zealanders will suffer from anxiety at some stage in their life.

I've written before about how I deal with anxiety in my life, which involves a great deal of checking in on my self, talking it out, meditation and sometimes pharmaceuticals.

When I am in the middle of an anxiety episode, which may be a panic attack, or just feeling totally freaked out or wanting to run away, I find the best thing for me is to take half a lorazepam and go to bed. Lorazepam is a strictly controlled benzodiazepine medication used to treat anxiety. I wake up the next day feeling a lot better and thankful that there was help available to me. I often wonder how we coped 100 years ago without readily available pharmaceuticals; I think the answer is we probably didn't.

I love to read about women in the early 1900s and have noticed it was common for society women like Nancy Mitford and Lady Cynthia

Asquith to get on the laudanum (a mixture of alcohol and morphine) when they needed to calm down. Every house had some.

These days we know that medication can have a downside too. It's better if we can help our anxiety in other ways because for some people, lorazepam and similar anxiety medication can be addictive.

The return of using psychedelics as a treatment for depression and anxiety is getting some good support these days. Psilocybin is derived from magic mushrooms. A recent study found that a group of people with depression fared better on psilocybin than the traditional SSRI antidepressants, which are a $15 billion industry.

Robin Carhart-Harris, head of the Centre for Psychedelic Research at Imperial College London, led the study and reported that while he suspected that psilocybin might perform well compared with the SSRI antidepressant, he had not expected it to perform as well as it did. People in the psilocybin group showed evidence of greater improvements across most measures of depression, as well as anxiety symptoms, work and social functioning, suicidal feelings and the ability to feel emotion and pleasure.

Further research has found that psilocybin could also help to treat drug and alcohol dependency and PTSD.

Since he released these findings, many countries are working to legalise psilocybin therapy, including Australia. In New Zealand, at the University of Auckland, an LSD microdosing trial was under way in 2020.

You may remember, as I do, that in the 1960s and '70s there was a moral panic about 'tripping', as it was called then, on either magic mushrooms or LSD (lysergic acid diethylamide). Concerns about the effect the drugs were having on young people led to them eventually being made illegal.

This was a shame because the many studies being done on these compounds and how they can help people were immediately shut down for 40 years. Now this research is being brought out into the light again, and proponents believe that psychedelics will soon become legal for therapeutic purposes.

I've never taken LSD or magic mushrooms, mainly because I believed the moral panic that went around at the time about bad trips and chewing your fingers off or something like that. I read *Christiane F.: Autobiography of a girl of the streets and heroin addict* when I was 19 and that put me off 'serious' drugs for life.

But in the future, I hope psychedelics could be a treatment we are all offered. I do love the way they are presented — you basically lie down in a peaceful setting, like a yoga studio, and are given the drug while listening to calming music. Guides check in on you every 15 minutes just in case you do become frightened or disoriented.

The trip usually lasts about six hours so it's a commitment, but studies are showing that in some cases just one trip is enough to have significant impacts on people's wellbeing.

I'd certainly be keen to give it a go.

Social biome

When I am dealing with a crisis, like my mother dying or my daughter being severely ill in hospital, I tend to shut down. I shut up shop and just don't communicate with anyone unless it's absolutely necessary. At times like these I just want to talk to my husband and my kids, who are my closest connections. My friends don't get a look-in — they know that I will go quiet and they wait. The only problem is that after a week or so I get shitty that my friends aren't checking in on how I'm coping, conveniently forgetting that for years I have taught them to stay away.

This is how I cope — it works for me. It's about setting a boundary. But when there isn't a crisis it is really important for your mental health to stay connected with people. It's called having a healthy social biome.

In a recent article in *The Guardian*, Robin Dunbar, a retired professor of anthropology and evolutionary psychology at the University of Oxford, said that people tend to think of their social world as mostly based on 'pair relationships'. But there is also 'an ever-expanding network called the family, the community, the nation, the globe, which is all highly interconnected,' he says.

He cites 'a huge torrent — a tsunami really' of epidemiological papers in the past 15 years showing that 'the best single predictor for your psychological wellbeing and health, for your physical wellbeing and health — even for your risk of dying — is the number and quality of friendships that you have.' A healthy social biome, he suggests, is key to a healthy body and mind.

This doesn't mean that you have to rush out and add more friends to your life. It just means you might want to spend more time with the friends and family you do have.

I've had to work on this a bit. I loved the Covid lockdowns. I absolutely loved them. I stayed connected with people by Zoom, email and text but I loved the isolation and having no pressure to be somewhere. I'm not alone; a lot of people have told me they had the same reaction.

But post Covid you can't go around pretending you are still in lockdown or you will become quite lonely.

Here are some ideas if you'd like to try to enhance and encourage your social biome:

- Get on the phone and talk to someone. These days I think we rely on text to communicate far too often. I liked the old days when the phone was connected to the wall. It sat there quietly minding its own business and knew its place. When there was a phone call, you did it the honour of sitting next to it — or lying on the floor, as I was fond of doing, for hour-long conversations with friends. You had a good old chat, during which nothing distracted you. The person you were speaking with had your full attention, then you hung up and went off to live your life.

- Embrace Zoom. It's nasty I know and we were all very uncomfortable when we started using it, but it is a good tool for connecting with people far away. Use it and stay connected.

- Don't be afraid to refresh old friendships, especially if you've let them slide a little. People are always glad to hear from you, but if it's your fault you haven't been present in the friendship — and I'm looking at myself here — make the effort to re-establish those bonds.

- Invite people out again. Paul and I used to have great big parties and dinners and lunches with our friends but somehow we stopped doing that as much, probably because we now live miles away from anyone. So it is up to us to make the effort when we are around our friends and family in Auckland to have that coffee, arrange an outing, make things happen. I even reached out to someone I had only met once after reading something she wrote about not having any women friends and suggested we could be friends and have a coffee. It hasn't happened yet but I'm glad I made the effort.

- 'I was just thinking of you' is a great way to remind your friend that you are still there and present. Fortunately I am blessed with having amazingly far-out, ridiculous dreams involving my friends so I will often send them a message and tell them all about it to make them laugh. If something makes me think of them — a passage I've read in a book or a picture I've seen — I'll send them that too. It's a relatively easy way of saying that they matter to you without having to go to too much effort!

- Go back to writing letters, but on email. My friend Kerre and I are both really busy. So we're not the kind of friends who check in with each other every day. Once we went for a few weeks not touching base, mainly because I was dealing with a sick daughter and had closed off. So she sent me an email. A nice, long, chatty email, much like a letter you would send in the old days, catching me up on all her news. I didn't want to chat on the phone so I sent one back. And now we email each other about twice a week and make each other laugh. I joke that one day we should publish those emails. This has become our way of staying connected because sometimes a phone call when you're busy is just too rushed to let you make a real connection.

Do something you never thought you'd do

People who are lonely and disconnected or unhappy are often told to 'go out there and get a hobby!' We are told to join a book club or a choir, or take up painting.

I always find that advice a bit wasted on me. I can't paint, I could think of nothing worse than someone disagreeing with what I thought about a book I had just read, and I used to sing in a choir at school but I'm not about to start again.

Instead I do stuff for fun. I'll get out my old sewing machine and sew a simple skirt or dress from some vintage fabric I have bought online.

As I was writing this book I became a guerrilla signwriter. We live near the Koutu Boulders, which are widely touted as a great thing to visit in the Hokianga. The problem is there are no signs telling the tourists where they are, which road to turn down to get to them, and not to drive on the beach unless you have a four-wheel drive.

We've had tourists climbing all over farmland looking for the boulders, which are actually on the beach. We've seen them driving down our road and getting stuck without ever seeing a boulder. We've had a lot of people on our doorstep expecting us to have a tractor to pull them out of the mud. We don't have one, so they have to hope the AA gets to them before the tide does.

Paul is the sort of person who believes in councils. He believes that if you pay your rates then you can ring the council and they will come and put up some helpful signs. He believed that for seven months while he talked to the council about putting up the signs, which would help the tourists who support our region with their tourist dollars. Then I decided that it wasn't going to happen. The man who came and looked wouldn't return Paul's calls. The man's boss who was always in a meeting or out of the office wouldn't return his calls either.

So when Paul was away in Auckland I decided to surprise him. I became a guerrilla signwriter, and made some signs and put them up. I broke the law but I really wanted to make my husband's day.

The signs weren't great. They looked like something my six-year-old self might have made, although my six-year-old self has just told me that they would have been much better because she had a set of metal stencils made by her grandfather.

I made my stencils out of paper using nail scissors and then painted them in with an eye make-up brush on bits of old pine I found around

the place, using some leftover blue paint from a bookshelf craft job. As a guerrilla signwriter I was woefully unprepared.

As I made them I thought of the many happy tourists they would help and what a wonderful public service I was doing.

I screwed them on to the posts and as I did a man drove past in his van, backed up, looked at the sign and made the correct turn towards the boulders. I waved happily. Yes, that was me!

Paul drove home and completely missed the signs, so that was disappointing. But we haven't had any crying, muddy women at the door for a while.

Making those signs was the most fun I've had in ages. It didn't particularly connect me with anyone but it was for a good cause, and it created a heap of positive vibes for me.

How to fail

We are taught as children that making a mistake is failure. It's now considered okay to fail — in fact it's a great thing to do.

I once interviewed English writer Elizabeth Day, who has a podcast called How to Fail, where she asks very famous and important people to name three failures. She told me that when she was setting up the podcast she could only get women to agree to be interviewed, because at first the men she approached just couldn't see that they had failed in life.

'Every single man I approached, apart from one person, said "I don't think I have failed. I'm not sure I'm right for this podcast." Whereas every single woman I approached said: "Oh my gosh I've failed so many times."'

Through her interviews, with people such as Phoebe Waller-Bridge, Kazuo Ishiguro, Nigel Slater, Marian Keyes and Graham Norton,

Elizabeth proves that talking about failure is a source of true strength and that failure can be a learning experience and something to value.

As a result of letting Elizabeth's podcast into my life, I have made time to list my failures and then see how they helped me in the long run.

In order to fail you have to put yourself out there, which is a whole other thing. JK Rowling hit the nail on the head when she said 'It is impossible to live without failing at something unless you live so cautiously that you might as well not have lived at all — in which case you fail by default.'

When I made the decision to stop editing *Thrive* magazine after seven issues, I wrote an editorial that talked about failure. I said:

> I have never stayed long at any of the magazines I have edited. In the days when I bothered to listen to my negative self-talk, I saw this as a failing. An inability to dig in and stay at the same job for decades. Instead I always found something else more interesting to do over there, around the corner, in another country.
>
> But when you need to keep yourself interested and engaged in life I think it's important to know what you need, when to do it and be brave enough to leap. To listen to that inner voice who is your cheerleader. Not to keep doing something because you fear people may criticise you.

I left *Thrive* in good shape and had some wonderful women on the cover, including Jacinda Ardern, Anika Moa and Dr Siouxsie Wiles, so by leaving it I was not failing. I felt so proud of myself that at the age of 58 I could still turn out a bloody good magazine. The story I wrote about Jacinda was one of the best I've ever written. If I hadn't put myself out there to do that job, which to be fair exhausted me and challenged me in ways I wasn't expecting, I would not have had that joy.

Get what you want

How many times have you walked into a meeting with your boss, or a discussion with your bank manager, and walked out without getting what you wanted?

If you think back on your conversation you may well find that you were too polite.

A few years ago I read a book by Chris Voss called *Never Split the Difference* and it changed my life. Chris is a former FBI negotiator, so he knows how to get the right answer from the person he is negotiating with. He knows how to get a positive result.

I read this book before a particularly complicated negotiation with my boss about my job. I knew that what I wanted would not be what he wanted. It wasn't a question of money, it was about prioritising lifestyle over hours.

I realised that in any communication I had with people in charge I had become what I had been taught to be: a woman asking nicely.

I would say 'Would it be possible?', 'Do you think it might be all right?', 'Would you be okay if I . . .?' Asking permission makes it really easy for someone to reply 'No.' You're actually encouraging them to say it.

I could also morph into a difficult bitch in my earlier days. I was a great door-slammer and purveyor of the one-line put-down as I stropped out of the room. I learned, eventually, that losing your shit and being deeply offensive doesn't actually get you what you want either.

Once I read Chris's book, I found that by turning things around I could actually get what I wanted.

I learned several techniques that I still use today — in fact I have these saved on my phone for ready reference.

- Before you even get started talking about what you want, listen to what the other person wants. This makes them feel relaxed and listened to.

- Practice tactical empathy. This means listening to what the other person is saying then saying it back to them. 'It sounds like you're really not comfortable with me working more from home.' This makes them feel heard.

- Slow the conversation down and use what Chris calls your 'late-night DJ voice'. If you talk slowly and meaningfully and don't resort to anger and emotion, you will be taken much more seriously.

- See if you can get the other person to say 'That's right' before you state what you want. This subconsciously gets them on your side. You could say 'I know that you and I both want this project to meet its target.' When they say 'That's right,' you are now a team.

- The most useful technique I found was to frame your request in a way that says 'This is going to happen.' So instead of saying 'Would it be okay with you, and feel free to say it's not, if I worked from home three days a week?', you would say 'I'm going to work from home three days a week, so let's sort out how we can make this work.'

I know that you are now thinking, well that's awfully bossy and presumptuous.

But it's not. It is clear communication stating what you want, rather than hiding it in clouds of female politeness and subservience.

Here's another example. Instead of saying 'I really think I'm worth more than that and even a small raise would make a huge difference to me,' say 'I'm going to earn more because I've proved to you that I'm worth it.' You may be scared that your boss might reply 'You're dreaming. Get out of here,' but I can pretty much guarantee they won't, because you are framing the conversation in a way that makes them feel like it would be a loss to turn you down.

Paul and I do a lot of negotiations with people by email and we always 'Chris Voss it'.

First we write the email, then we review it and take out all the pleading words that still creep in, even after two years of practice. Instead we just state simple sentences.

Most of the time it works, and sometimes it doesn't. But when it doesn't work then you can walk away from that negotiation knowing you did your best, and you are probably better off looking elsewhere for what you need to be happy.

Do nothing

In one of my earlier books, I advised women who were busy to find more time by simply not watching television. I reasoned that it was four hours per day (on average) that you can spend on yourself by having a long bath, going for a walk, having an early night, reading a book, doing some yoga — that sort of thing.

Since I wrote those words the smartphone has arrived and so we carry the equivalent of a TV screen around with us all the time. Most of us sign up to social media accounts like Facebook, Twitter and Instagram, which are designed to keep us engaged, checking in regularly, all day

every day from the moment we wake up to the moment we go to bed.

According to the tracking app Moment, the average American spends four hours a day staring at their smartphones. I'd guess that here in New Zealand we have similar usage hours.

A recent study in the UK by their broadcasting watchdog Ofcom found that adults spent an average of five hours and 40 minutes a day watching TV, which was up on any previous studies. The increase was blamed on the emergence of Netflix and the emerging tendency to binge-watch shows.

Google has noted that 'mobile devices loaded with social media, email and news apps' create 'a constant sense of obligation, generating unintended personal stress'.

When did you last sit down with someone for a coffee, a meal or a chat and not have both your phones sitting on the table like expectant babies waiting for their next feed?

So let's take the four hours of television and add another four hours across the day of checking in on our social media and emails.

I started getting quite resentful of the time I spent scrolling through Instagram when I found myself once again lying on the couch looking at recipes, pretty kittens and puppies and photos of Italy when I could have been reading a book or talking to someone. Recipes, pretty kittens and puppies and photos of Italy will always be available so why did I need to have a constant diet of them, several times a day?

I was also starting to get annoyed by some people I followed on Instagram. It wasn't their fault — it was their Instagram account, after all — but I found some of the stuff they were posting was a bit off. Instagram had gone from something pretty to something quite shouty where people found it necessary to parade and fluff their feathers. People I previously quite liked turned out to be quite different when they were shouting, and this upset me.

Some of it I think was due to Covid forcing people to reveal their true colours. A number of people I followed shouted about how we shouldn't be in lockdown and how herd immunity was the way to go and how unfair it was that their privileged lives were being inconvenienced.

I was shocked, as previously I'd thought these people were pretty cool and sort of on my wavelength.

If I unfollowed them that would be rude so I started just muting them, which is a polite way of not looking at their posts without offending them.

Then I realised that it was all just a horrible charade created by this beast. Not only was Instagram wasting my time, it was introducing social difficulties into my life. Muting someone on social media is no different to turning the other way when you pass someone on the street. It's rude. And I was doing it a lot.

I had deleted my Facebook and Twitter accounts years ago, mainly because of trolls, but I held on to Instagram because it showed me pretty pictures of things I was interested in, but slowly and surely it turned into something I felt I had to do. I needed to check in on my friends and family several times a day and make sure I liked all their posts so that they knew I cared and I also had to post some stuff on my page every few days to keep the 3000 people who were following me happy and engaged.

Then one day I had had enough. Did anyone really care? Did I really care? I looked at the piles of books beside my bed waiting to be read, the garden waiting for me to tend it, my work waiting for me to meet a deadline and I realised that lying on the couch swiping a phone had taken priority over things that bring me real, authentic and genuine joy. I had somehow persuaded myself that time with my phone was a recreational activity when it wasn't. It was an attention-hungry device, designed to keep me engaged and therefore making money for large corporations through the ads that I scrolled through and sometimes read, and it was doing this to the detriment of my quality of life. So I put my Instagram on hold — just to see what happened.

Nothing happened, which was sort of the point. And months later only two people had been in touch to say 'Why aren't you on Instagram any more?' One was my publisher, who was just checking that I was okay, and the other was someone who followed me from Australia and was worried I had blocked her. She messaged Paul and when he explained it was nothing personal, she said she missed my posts, which was nice. So my need to post every few days to keep 3000 people happy was obviously all in my head.

As a side note, if my Instagram account revives itself when this book is published I apologise for the blatant self-promotion, but in this world marketing through social media is essential if you want a book to be read.

Shortly after pausing the very needy Instagram, I read a book by Jenny Odell called *How to Do Nothing: Resisting the attention economy.*

To be honest I just read the first part of the title *How to Do Nothing* and thought it would be a self-help book from the US that would have tips and summaries to flick through — I'm quite a good speed-reader after years proofing magazines — and that I would take away one or two things that could help me embrace a less hectic lifestyle.

I took the book to Wellington with me where I had a board meeting to attend, some time at the opera with my friend Sue Kedgley, and a catch-up planned with my daughter Pearl, who lives there and works in parliament for the Green Party.

When I arrived, Wellington was in a blind panic because a man from Sydney had arrived with Covid, so everything was shut down to Level 2. The surrealist exhibition at Te Papa and the opera I had been planning to enjoy were both closed. I had an afternoon where it was just me in a nice hotel with hotel sheets and a lovely, fresh book to read. What woman doesn't love that?

I settled in, put a Spotify playlist called *Baroque for Thinking and Study* on the Bluetooth speaker and began to read.

I realised pretty quickly that this was not a US self-help book I could speed-read in an hour. It was a carefully researched, thoughtfully written book by a socially conscious artist in California. Jenny argues that by turning against social media or the 'attention economy' and clearing space by listening, thinking and spending time in nature, your local park or your own home, you cannot exactly do nothing, but you can do better things with your time.

As I read the pages I suddenly became aware that I was NOT CONCENTRATING. I was constantly putting down the book to check this or that, then I would return to the book for a few more pages. So I took out my notebook and pen, which I had near me to take notes about the book, and wrote a list of what I had spent that first hour doing. Here it is:

- I googled how much the Bose Bluetooth speaker in my room cost as I'd quite like to buy another one for travelling and it had a nice bass sound I really appreciated.

- I texted my kids — we have five — so that was five texts just saying that I was checking in and hoping they were having a nice day.

- I called my friend Kerre to check in on her weekend.

- I called Paul to tell him about the Bose speaker and how good it was and tell him how Kerre's weekend was going.

- I replied to the text replies from my kids.

- I cleaned my reading glasses, which involved a long search to find the cleaning solution and cloth — which were hiding at the bottom of my backpack.

- I made a coffee, which involved working out how to use the Nestlé capsule machine as well as having quite the dialogue in my head about those capsules filling landfills and how if I was really a greenie I would refuse to use it, but then I would have to go out for coffee and I didn't have my reusable cup with me so that's even more non-recyclable waste . . .

- I checked the time . . . four times.

- I googled nearby cafés that I might want to visit for a late lunch and then looked at their menus online.

- I also checked the room-service menu in case that would suffice.

- I noticed one of my nails was chipped so went looking for one of those sandpaper nail files you sometimes get in hotel bathrooms but couldn't find one.

- I made a supermarket shopping list for when I got home, which included a nail file.

- I wrote a few reminders for the following week, which included planting roses, adding some more lettuce seedlings to the lettuce patch and seeing if I could work out how to make a pumpkin and cashew curry using the pumpkin that had secretly grown in my garden, which I discovered just before I left.

- I googled pumpkin cashew curry recipes and saved a few on my phone.

- I checked my email five times. It was a Sunday. No one emails me on a Sunday any more.

What I found myself doing in that hotel room was repeating behaviours I had become quite used to during the past six months. Constant phone checking for Instagram or emails, constant looking up things on Google, constant queries and questions, all the time. Even on a Sunday. At one stage while working for *Thrive* I even installed an email blocker that only let me read emails three times a day. My habit of checking constantly had become uncontrollable — a symptom I later realised came from a job that wasn't for me.

I sat on the bed and laughed at the irony of what I was doing. I was trying to read a book about how to stop the very behaviour I was exhibiting while reading the book.

I put on my raincoat and took a walk on a wet, windy Wellington Sunday afternoon and then I came back and tried again.

This time it worked. What I learned from Jenny's book is that 'doing nothing' is actually not about doing nothing. She explains it as 'a kind of deprogramming device' and 'as sustenance for those feeling too disassembled to act meaningfully'.

She suggests that finding time to think, reflect, heal and sustain will repair ourselves. And then we need to relearn some behaviours. One of them is learning how to listen. She writes: 'Unfortunately, our constant engagement with the attention economy means that this is something many of us (myself included) may have to relearn . . . the platforms that we use to communicate with each other do not encourage listening. Instead they reward shouting and over-simple reaction.'

Jenny used the rose garden in her local park to sit and listen. She began to bird-watch and she walked away from social media, preferring #NOMO to #FOMO (the necessity of missing out instead of the fear of missing out).

When I finally finished the book that Sunday afternoon I realised that I was halfway there. Living in the Hokianga in a rural setting means that I am in touch with a lot of the things that help us do nothing. I spend time in nature every day. I know the names of all the birds that live around me and stop and listen to them often. I swim in the sea and am very attuned to the rhythms of nature such as winds and tides as I literally immerse myself in them. I rest my mind regularly with meditation, breathing practices and good sleep.

But instead of prioritising all these things in my life, they always came second. The minute work got in the way, they were edged out of my week.

'Work' has always meant 'money' to me. When you're raising five children you always need money, so I prioritised that from when I had my first child at the age of 24. So I'd spent 34 years saying yes to jobs that stressed me out. Although, if I'm honest, I also loved most of them and am eternally grateful that journalism was a rewarding career for me.

In my late fifties I am lucky to need less money to support our children, who are all adults now. I needed to see that it would be possible not to make work my number one.

After I left my editor's job at *Thrive*, Paul and I went to see a money advisor to see how the next 30 years might look for us. Our advisor asked me what I wanted to see happening in the next year.

My answer was swift and forthright. 'In a few weeks someone is going to offer me another big job and I want to be able to hear myself say "no", instead of saying "yes" like I have always done.'

He asked me why I said 'yes' all the time and I replied 'Because I've always had to,' but also, if I'm honest, I love a good challenge.

I think he thought I was dreaming about another job offer so we proceeded to plan our lives unencumbered by Wendyl's serial and annoying job offers.

A few weeks later I was offered another job.

My reply was to send the book cover of *How to Do Nothing*, but I didn't say no. I didn't say yes either. I said 'I'll think about it,' and made appointments with our money advisor and my therapist. Then I harassed my children and friends asking them what to do. They, of course, just wanted me to do what felt right for me, which did nothing to help me make my decision.

Then the good old *New Zealand Woman's Weekly* got in touch to see if I was free to do some writing. I had edited the *Weekly* in the late nineties and my Green Goddess column had run in it for over a decade before the Bauer closures. When the *Weekly* returned with a new owner I was one of the many people throughout New Zealand who were very relieved to have our iconic magazine back.

The first story they wanted me to do was an interview with Dame Kiri Te Kanawa. Before I knew it I was in Auckland sitting across from this wonderful woman telling me about how she had moved home to New Zealand to be with her grandson.

I drove away from that interview and felt a feeling of pure joy wash over me. I realised I had come full circle and was writing celebrity profile pieces just as I did 40 years ago when I was 20 and interviewing Bono from U2. I was back where I began and loving every minute of it.

So I turned down the big job and now I write profile pieces for the

Weekly and a column for my local newspaper, *The Northern Advocate*, which I love. There isn't a week that goes by when I haven't enjoyed myself immensely chatting to someone interesting and writing up their story or writing about some local issue I feel passionate about.

I have finally found myself able to say that simple word: no.

The great escape

Every time you use social media, Google or Spotify, an algorithm starts tracking you. It takes note of every site you visit and starts assembling content to show you targeted advertising as well as music or recipes you might like. The idea is that by showing you stuff you are interested in, you might click on it or even buy it, and that means a payment goes to the content provider.

My biggest issue with how we use the internet these days is that it closes us out from the other stuff that is in the world. We become enclosed in our own little bubble full of all the things we like. To me, that is stifling.

As an example, on Spotify I often listen to James Taylor, Van Morrison, Carole King, Joni Mitchell plus a bit of jazz, some country, and a lot of blues and classical.

Spotify now makes playlists for me based on what I might like to listen to, so I end up listening to pretty much the same thing every day — which means I never get to hear new music. That's only happened since I began streaming music. (In Spotify's defence it does also put up 'new music' playlists but I never click on them.)

As a child in the sixties I remember going to bed every night with my little turquoise battery radio under my pillow. It was tuned to Radio Hauraki and I would hear so many amazing songs and loved every one of them.

As I grew up I went to concerts and listened to lots of different bands as we entered the punk era. I still get quite emotional when I occasionally get to be in a pub and a band is playing. I love that so much and it happens so rarely now.

In those days even if you went to see the same band play several times a month, they would always introduce new material and you might love it or hate it. But at least you were exposed to it.

When I was 20 I talked my way off the news desk at *The Auckland Star* and into a job as a 'rock reporter', which meant I went to a lot of gigs. That's when my love of live music really hit its stride. I was out every night with a whisky in one hand, a fag in the other and listening to all the amazing music that New Zealand bands, and often international bands too, had to offer.

I would go to friends' flats and they would put on a new (vinyl) album and we would all sit and listen to the whole thing, exposing ourselves to not just the hits but everything else in between. There were no phones or text conversations to look at — instead, we would sit and concentrate on the music, chatting a bit, but mainly listening.

On Sunday nights my whole flat would gather around the TV and we would watch *Radio with Pictures*. We were completely absorbed by what we were seeing and hearing, often for the first time, then the next day someone in the flat would go out and buy the record.

When I was working at the *Star* I remember heading home early one day with a record that had been dropped on my desk. I arrived at my flat in Parnell, the sun was shining through the window and I placed the album on the turntable, lit a fag and sat back in my favourite old armchair to listen. I wasn't multi-tasking — no cooking, reading, or talking on the phone. I was just sitting in the sun with the full expectation that I would listen to some music. Who does that any more?

The music started and I was completely absorbed. You might

think I was listening to the Rolling Stones or The Beatles for the first time. I was listening to club music. Frankie Goes to Hollywood's 'Relax'. I loved it so much I kept playing it for days. The mere fact that I had found something new and exciting to listen to made me very, very happy.

Today, how do we ever hear new music? We are too comfortable in our own bubble of 'what we like' fed to us by radio stations that play the hits and streaming services that use algorithms, so we never have that moment where we hear something and think, Wow that's different and I love it.

When today's Frankie Goes to Hollywood turns up there's a good chance I will never hear it because it's club music and I don't listen to that on Spotify. I also don't go to clubs.

Occasionally my kids will send me links to music that is new and interesting and I love them for that. But mainly Spotify just hands me stuff it knows I'll like.

To me it's like going into a book shop and only being allowed to look at the books on healthy living because those are the books you bought last time you were in that shop. Imagine that? Or going to your favourite clothing shop and only being allowed to look at jeans because last time you were there you bought jeans.

This seems outrageous, but this is exactly what is happening to you in every aspect of your life that you share on the internet.

And that is the main reason I gave up social media. I want to keep exposing myself to new stuff, whether it is music, politics, people or books. I just want to properly live in the world and absorb all of it, not just what my phone feeds to me. Some of what I'm being exposed to might upset me if I don't like it or agree with it, but at least I know about it and experience it and think about it and make up my mind about it. And some of it surprises me with such joy, just like my discovery of Frankie Goes to Hollywood.

Resisting social media

I remember the thrill of social media when it all began. I was an enthusiastic Twitter user and was named by the *Herald* as one of the top Twitter accounts to follow. I used Facebook a lot too, and enjoyed how it connected me to people overseas, friends and family, some new people — and who hasn't searched up old boyfriends? I found it very interesting to see what these people were up to because I'm nosy.

Then I realised that it was just too intrusive for me and I started to read articles that detailed the hidden cost of social media.

Facebook, Google, Twitter and TikTok recently signed a pledge, led by the World Wide Web Foundation (WWWF), to fix persistent weaknesses in how they tackle online gender-based violence. More than a third of women worldwide have experienced abuse online, and for younger women that rises to almost half, according to a 2021 study from the Economist Intelligence Unit. The four tech companies have pledged to tackle that abuse by focusing on two major areas of concern across their platforms: the inability to control who can reply, comment on and engage on posts; and the lack of clear and reliable reporting systems for flagging online abuse.

Social media is no friend to women. It exposes us to trolls and tormentors. That was certainly my experience on Facebook and Twitter simply because I have opinions and I'm not afraid to voice them. As a friend once told me, 'You don't know how to keep your mouth shut.' So you can imagine what the people who don't like me say.

It brings out the worst in people and provides a platform for anonymous cowards whose one aim in life is to upset others at no cost to themselves. We're not just talking disagreeable comments here, we're talking death threats and abuse. I think that is evil and I don't want to support any platform that allows that to happen to women.

It also disconnects us from reality while connecting us to unrealistic goals. Haven't we all watched as someone decides to become an influencer in their own Instagram world and fails miserably?

Social media targets us with relentless advertising — when we use it we are under continual surveillance, prodded by algorithms run by some of the richest corporations in the world.

It also takes us away from human connection with our family and friends. How many times have you watched a family out at dinner with everyone on their phones? I recently saw a family of four in an airport where the two parents and two children all had their earphones in and were watching their separate screens in complete silence. Maybe it was a rare occurrence — I was only witnessing a snapshot in time — but it struck me as an interesting way to have a family holiday.

I've also seen couples out at dinner staring at their phones instead of talking. Paul and I will take our phones out to dinner but they remain in my handbag and in his pocket. We will check them if we're waiting on something for work or there is something urgent, but apart from that we talk to each other and enjoy our food, just like the old days. How weird that we have to prioritise that now.

It also takes away our freedom to just sit. In a chair. In the sun. That's it. Just sit there and maybe listen to music, or chat with your partner or watch the sun as it puts itself to bed and listen to the birds as they too settle in for the night.

If you're reading this and thinking, Oh that's not me, that's just Wendyl, then take my advice and activate a screen-time tracker. If you have an iPhone it's there in Settings or you can download an app. Just track how often you stare at your phone over a week and which apps are taking all your time and for how long.

Then tell me you're okay with that.

You can also put your account on hold for a while and see how you go. You'll find it's very difficult to actually delete your Facebook or Instagram account so you'll have to google how to do that when the time comes. But it's easy enough to put it on hold, so do that and see how it feels. You may find you don't miss it at all.

Just for you

When you find a bit of time on your hands because you're giving social media a rest, it's a good idea to dig out those things you love doing but can never find the time for. Mostly this is described as hobbies, but that's not what I'm talking about.

For years I have read two newspapers, *The Times* and *The Guardian*, on my iPad in bed first thing. I like overseas press because there is some fine writing in those newspapers, the likes of which you no longer see in the local newspaper offerings. I particularly like the feature writing and the columns but I also scan the news, which means I'm always up to date with the UK if you ever need an expert.

Usually my two newspaper readings take about an hour — I have my cup of tea, read the papers and then get up and into the world.

As a journalist I get a lot of joy from reading good journalism but this is also valuable time. Many of the books or articles quoted in this book came out of reading about them in my UK papers. I rarely finish my morning newspaper session without jotting down notes about this or that, or books I need to read.

One of the best days writing this book was when I worked out how to pull up all of the *Times* and *Guardian* articles I had sent to my email and had since forgotten about. There were hundreds of them. I had been researching the topic of caring for years and it was all there waiting for me in my email inbox. Joy.

When I gave up social media I added two more papers to my list, *The New York Times* and *The Washington Post*. Both have excellent iPad apps.

Now my morning read takes two hours and neatly absorbs some of the time I used to spend on social media. I am lucky that I can spend two hours a day reading newspapers as I'm not having to get up and go into an office to work a full day. This is the greatest gift I can give myself on a daily basis — reading well-written words that inform me intelligently. There's no celebrity gossip, insane right-wing nonsense (well occasionally in *The Times*), badly written columns by NewstalkZB hosts or conspiracy theories.

On Mondays I will admit that I spend most of the morning reading the papers because I'm reading the Sunday editions and they always have lovely, huge features and lifestyle sections that I adore.

Not so long ago I would have felt guilty reading the papers all morning on a Monday, but I don't any more. I've been a journalist for nearly 40 years and I think I've earned the right to read good journalism and spend my Monday morning immersed in it.

Learning to listen

When we're engaged in the shouty world of social media, it can be hard to listen when you need to. We become so focused on telling our story and so used to having a silent audience that doesn't respond or stop you going on and on that we forget to pause, listen and let someone else hold the talking stick for a while.

Being a good listener can be a gift to yourself and others. At face value, sitting comfortably and listening to someone talk about themselves can bring you some wonderful stories and teach you things. To listen you need to be genuinely interested and curious about what the other person

is saying. That means sitting and looking at them, not looking over their shoulder or off into the distance. I find when I am genuinely listening to someone my body language changes. I lean forward in my seat and I concentrate on their face and body language. It's as if all my senses are slowing down and focusing on this person in the hope that I'll absorb everything that is being said. Every time I interview someone, this is how I am.

I once did an online course on Zoom that was about writing a novel. It was called 'Writing Action: The Emotional and Dramatic Moment' and there were something like 60 of us on that Zoom call.

I was excited to do this two-hour course and I was ready to listen, properly, because I admired the person who was taking the course and I knew I could learn from her.

Unfortunately, the chat function on Zoom was left open and so our tutor was constantly distracted by the comments being made by the 60 participants. Most of the comments added nothing to the dialogue and seemed to be designed to say 'Look at me, I'm here, I'm important,' or perhaps that was just the case with the former National Party MP who was chatting up a storm.

The constant stopping and addressing the comments in the chat box by our tutor prevented me from listening. I kept losing my train of thought and ended up being really frustrated and annoyed. I hadn't paid a lot of money for the privilege of reading 60 other people's opinions on the emotional and dramatic moment, but if I had, I would have demanded a refund.

This, to me, is a classic example of people being unable to listen any more. I also see this in meetings where there is always one person, usually a man in my experience, who cannot shut up.

In large meetings where there will be conflict or disagreement, such as union/employer negotiations, there will always be one person from the union who sits in the meeting and deliberately says nothing. Their job is to simply listen to everything everyone says and take notes. Because when you're not competing for the talking stick, you notice a lot more than those who are.

When you do listen, you give yourself a huge gift of knowledge, sometimes humour, and sometimes just the joy of hearing another person's voice.

But where listening really becomes caring is when you give someone the gift of listening to their problems and giving them a place where they can safely talk to someone they trust.

The Guardian's agony aunt Annalisa Barbieri wrote an article about how she learned to listen.

'Listening, I discovered, wasn't just about waiting for the other person to stop talking, or asking good questions, or even not interrupting. It was about really hearing what the other person was saying, and why they were saying it. Being interested, but also curious. Sometimes that means looking for what's not said, what's left out, which words are used to mask emotions that are hard to acknowledge. Likewise, good listening is about approaching what has been said as if you've never heard it before. Put simply, it's about paying attention.'

When you are good with words, it's easy to express your feelings and your opinions in a group dynamic. But many people find it hard to find the right words, to express themselves in neat sentences and sound bites. And if you listen in a group dynamic, you will soon see that some people just never get heard, yet they are fascinating people with interesting lives. How sad that you never heard their take on the topic you were discussing.

I have worked on my listening skills as a way of helping other people. Here's what I've learned:

- It's okay to leave a silence while the other person battles to find the right words, or is overcome with emotion. It is fine to just sit together and wait. You do not need to fill the gap.

- If you're hearing something difficult or challenging, such as a toddler having a meltdown or someone close to you telling you something that hurts you, don't respond in anger. It's so easy to respond with 'Well, you might think that but quite frankly you're just as bad,' or something defensive designed to take the pressure off you. Instead, take what they've said and say it back to them. 'I can see that you are finding this really hard.' They will agree with you and then, and only then, you can say 'What can I do to help/change/make you feel better?'

- Don't immediately respond with your own experience of what they are telling you. They don't care if you, too, had a relationship break-up. You are there to hear about their experience, not pepper it with your own. By doing this you are steering the conversation away from them before they've had a chance to talk it out. This happened to me in an extraordinary way shortly after my daughter Virginia died of cot death. My first husband and I were invited around to some friends for dinner. We were told that they knew how we felt because their dog had died a few months ago. I looked at my husband, and we made our excuses and left.

- Don't resort to platitudes that you think will make them feel better. 'Everything happens for a reason', 'Life's funny isn't it?' or my favourite, 'Maybe this is meant to be.' Someone once said that to me about Virginia's death, and added that 'God called

her back to heaven.' I didn't hit him but I nearly did — luckily a
friend saved me by leaping in and telling him to piss off. These
platitudes merely say that you're not actually listening, you're just
pretending to listen and you're not at all interested in helping.

- Be patient and practise compassion. People who are upset will
  be repetitive, especially if they feel they aren't being heard. They
  may also be amazingly self-pitying, especially if no one has
  listened to them before now.

- Don't rush. You might have only allowed an hour in your busy
  day for this coffee but suddenly it's turned into a real-life drama
  complete with several plot twists. Be kind, and if you can't shift
  your next appointment, at least offer to follow up again soon
  and make the time to be present for as long as they need.

- Ask reflective questions. So instead of 'Oh man I would have
  been so angry about that,' try saying 'It sounds like you felt
  really angry about that.' Remember, it's not about you.

- Children and teenagers are really good at using dismissive
  language if they can't find the words. 'I don't care', 'It doesn't
  matter', 'Just forget it' are not true statements. They are simply
  saying 'This is too hard, help me.' A good way to keep them
  talking is to say 'I can feel that you do care, maybe we could break
  it down a bit and look at the bits you feel you can talk about now.'

- Be trustworthy and safe to talk to. I had to really work hard
  at this with my kids. They knew that everything they told me
  would be passed on to Paul, because he is my backup on all

things. So I had to start saying 'Are you okay if I talk to Paul about it?', and so far none of the kids have said no. But you need to make sure the person you are listening to knows that it goes no further unless you ask for permission to tell someone else. This establishes a lovely bond of trust and you will be able to help a lot more.

- Teenagers really appreciate not having to look you in the eye. I've had some of my most truthful conversations with my kids when we were on road trips. Some people are more comfortable telling you stuff if you're not staring at them.

- Watch your facial reactions. My counsellor is so good at masking her reactions when she hears me tell her things. Sometimes she will burst into laughter if I've told her something funny but mostly she has the same face on for the whole session. When we're dealing with difficult stuff we look at the other person to judge how they are taking the news. If your face is screwed up in disgust, that's going to shut down the conversation. So try to be open and bland. I will say, though, that after 30 years with my counsellor I have noticed that her eyes flicker ever so slightly when I tell her some things. This usually means, in my experience, that she knows something about that subject or person. Knowing this is of no use to me, but I like looking out for it just the same.

- Go into a listening session with the full intention to just listen. Expect to not be listened to at all; that is fine because you are giving of yourself and caring for this person. When you need to be listened to, find a counsellor or give someone these tips to read.

By my own admission, I'm not a great listener but I'm working on it. I try not to interrupt my husband or kids when they are telling me something, but sometimes I do. I try not to interrupt my friends when they are telling me stories, but sometimes I do. I am really trying to get better, and when I do interrupt, I'm very aware that I am and that I need to try harder.

Not coping

Guess what? Not coping is okay. I was brought up to believe that you always put on a front, best foot forward, never show weakness. When I was first diagnosed with depression when I was 32, my mother told me to never, ever tell anyone.

'Don't tell your friends, your boss, or anyone because You Will Be Judged.'

So I didn't. I took the antidepressants and a month later I felt better and got on with life.

Only later did I realise that my mother was talking from experience. She struggled all her life to present herself as someone living a good life and not at all mentally ill, and as a result lived her whole life on Valium topped up with alcohol.

I wish I had told some people back then because it would have made it a lot easier to get through those dark times, as well as the ones that followed.

Then slowly people started talking, thanks to a lot of work by the Mental Health Foundation. As a community we began to take away the stigma that had been associated with depression and anxiety.

This was really important, especially for women. In the past, if we didn't conform to standards deemed to be normal, we were dismissed

as mad, and put in mental asylums for the simple reason that we were causing havoc for men.

Today things are still tough for some women who are dismissed as being 'loo loo la la' just because they are struggling to conform to a social norm that has been set by the people around them.

For women I think it is much harder to take to your bed, shut the door and ask that you be left alone with your thoughts in an effort to recover. We are often the person running everything and our absence is felt by others who feel that we are letting them down. So many of us just keep going out of guilt when we actually need to look after ourselves so that when we are up and running again we are feeling okay.

On a very simple level, not coping is your mind and body saying it's time to do some self-care.

For some people addiction gets in the way of accessing that message. Alcohol and drugs can provide a wonderful dimming effect on trauma. How often have we said after a hard day at work, or a long day with nightmare kids: 'God, I need a drink!'

It makes sense to find something that relaxes you. The very act of holding a full glass of wine becomes a signal that it's okay to stop, sit on the couch and just recover.

But for some people it's not just a glass of wine, it's a night of wine, or drugs, or whatever they use. I talk about this more in a later chapter, but for now I'll just say that covering your mind with the cottonwool of drugs and alcohol means it's harder to see what you actually need.

The problem with addiction is that it ends up taking more of that chosen drug to work and then it affects your life and other people's lives too. Sometimes you hit rock bottom and hopefully there is someone there who loves you and will not give up on you, because that is the key to keeping addicted loved ones alive. Never, ever leave them unless their actions are causing you harm, in which case you need to protect yourself first. But if you're a friend or a parent or a child who feels they are able to help that person get into recovery, then you must never give up.

For other people dancing with addiction, there's nothing in the way of getting help except perhaps a sense of denial and a hatred of conflict. For those people, it's a great idea to find a good therapist they trust to help peel away the layers constructed over the years to keep themselves safe. I know that for some people a private therapist is just too expensive, but talk to your GP and see if you can access some funding. Your GP will be able to recommend local therapists for your particular situation, and they may know of some who are cheaper than others.

I found my therapist through my GP.

Once you have peeled back a few of those layers, you can then see what you need to do to care for yourself going forward, to be rid of the things that cause you to be unhappy and unstable.

I have been in therapy for 30 years, with the same therapist. These days I only see her about once a year. It's not a scheduled visit — I just make an appointment when I feel like it, usually around December, and she looks at her notes and says 'So last time I saw you was about a year ago.' Obviously December is the month when I evaluate how things are going for my mental health.

Once after some particularly tough work, she looked at me at the end of our session and said 'I think you don't need to see me any more. I think you've done the work now.'

I looked at her in horror. I had become dependent on her, so she was doing what good therapists do. She had done her job and was now sending me off to cope on my own.

Once I was over the shock I jokingly said 'So I'm healed now? I'll never get depressed again?'

To which she replied 'Life isn't like that. You never know what's around the next corner.'

And she was right. You can do the work, but then something comes up and you need to keep doing the work when it needs to be done. The skill is being able to realise when things feel rough and get the help you need.

Finding a therapist is tough, so don't give up. I've met some terrible therapists as well as some very good ones. I'll tell you what I know about choosing a therapist — if you ring up and get an appointment the next day that isn't the result of a cancellation, that's not good. You want someone who is in demand.

Do ask around. If you know someone who is also in therapy ask them who they see and why. I've recommended my therapist to many, many people over the years, but not all of them clicked with her because it's a very individual thing. Also my therapist doesn't work with addiction issues, which cuts out half the people I sent to her.

If you are in a therapy session and feel uncomfortable, unable to share, your therapist talks too much and doesn't listen, or even if you don't like what they're wearing, don't keep going. You need to really trust the person you are talking to and feel comfortable sharing some pretty rough stuff. Ask yourself how you'd feel bursting into tears and shuddering with emotion in front of them. If the answer is you'd feel okay, then you've probably found a good therapist for you. If the answer is no, then move on. Most people talk with a few therapists before they find one that works for them.

It's also a good idea to check the therapist's qualifications and see that they belong to a reputable organisation that has codes and ethics.

It's also okay not to get therapy. Some people, who by their own admission are not doing well, are obviously messing up their lives. It is tempting to suggest they get some therapy, but they probably won't. That has to be okay. For some people the time isn't right, or they just can't face the hard work that therapy demands, so they choose to continue on with their life slightly unhinged. Your job as a friend or a loved one is to accept them as they are, now. One day they may take the step, or they may not. Pressuring them will not work.

Some people include a regime in their lives to give themselves the care they need. These people practise yoga and meditation, go on retreats, or practise mindfulness. People do many, many things to keep themselves on an even keel and while some of it may seem a bit woo-woo to you, it's not to others, so respect that they are doing it for their mental health.

These days there is a lot of help online for whatever you need. There are some great resources over at the Mental Health Foundation. There are wonderful psychologists available online and you can also tune into some great podcasts. I've listed a few of my favourites at the end of this book.

But do be wary. Some podcasts can go really deep and you may find that you get triggered. If this happens, therapy has taught me to take some deep breaths, then concentrate and isolate the feeling. Work out what it is related to, then name it, pull it out and re-examine it and then tell it to go away. In my mind I mentally put it in an imaginary shoebox under the bed and then I move on.

Later when I'm feeling a bit better I'll bring it out and tap it away using Thought Field Therapy, again taught to me by my therapist. You can hook into great apps for tapping these days so maybe give that a go.

That can be quite hard work, so I try to stay alert for anything triggering so I can protect myself from it.

Once I was at a dinner when a woman I barely knew became over-inquisitive about something that had happened to me in my life. She kept going on and on about it, wanting me to share my experience. Fortunately I hadn't been drinking, otherwise the outcome might have been worse because I find anger takes a very free rein when alcohol is involved.

But I did put up my hand in a 'stop now' gesture and said, quite sternly, 'If you don't mind, I'd rather not talk about this now.'

She was a bit taken aback but did as she was asked, and I switched the conversation to my love of roses.

Triggering is an overused word but it's one I respect. It's defined as causing a strong emotional reaction of fear or worry, because someone is made to remember something upsetting that has happened in the past. For example, I can be triggered by something I'm watching — so I avoid shows about babies or children who die.

It can also be finding yourself in a situation that reminds you of something that happened in the past. When my mother died and I was cleaning out her belongings, the smell of her triggered feelings of trauma and I felt nauseous.

If you have some trauma, and most people do, then it pays to be aware of people, places or stories that could trigger you.

A friend who had listened to the same podcast that had triggered me had the same thing happen to her, so that made me feel a little less vulnerable. But there I go again. There is nothing wrong with being vulnerable or having issues.

Sometimes my husband gets triggered by a movie that reminds him of how he felt as a seven-year-old boy when his mother died. His reaction is so admirable. He sits there and cries his eyes out. Then he's fine. I love that he can be so open and allow that emotion to just come right out and show itself. This is an example of knowing what you need to do and not trying to close it down or cover it up because of what society expects of you, which, as we all know, is 'men don't cry'.

The important thing is that a good podcast will really help, but do tread carefully and don't be afraid to stop it if things get weird.

Body

Our lives have been changed by Covid-19. Most of the talk about those changes is negative, despite the fact that we live in New Zealand and had one of the best Covid responses in the world.

So let's talk about a positive. Many of us are now actually caring about our bodies and making an effort to feed and exercise them properly.

I feel that in years gone by, many of us have ignored our bodies, throwing any old stuff into them, and then been surprised when they let us down by getting cancer or heart disease.

We abuse our bodies with too much alcohol, introduce them to fast food that has very little valuable nutrition, glug down endless soft drinks full of sugar, overwork them, don't get enough good sleep, and think it'll be okay.

Back in the day we smoked a lot too. Not once did we stop and say to ourselves 'Hold on a minute, this thing you walk around in needs good nutrition to power itself and ultimately keep you alive. Maybe you need to look at what you're doing to it.'

I think for many years we disassociated ourselves from our bodies and thought very little about them except to criticise how they looked.

When I was first pregnant in 1986, it never occurred to me to improve my eating or even look at a nutrition plan. Nor did my doctor suggest it. I just got pregnant and made a baby. I knew enough to give up alcohol and smoking, which I did, but I ate whatever I felt like. I do remember having a massive need to eat croissants.

Post Covid, the health of our bodies might well be the difference between dying from a deadly virus or surviving it. Being healthy — particularly having a strong immune system and being a reasonable weight — so that our bodies can function well has become a focus for many of us, including me.

For years I have written about body image and how we need to just accept ourselves. I still believe that.

But post Covid we have learned a few things. Statistics gathered during the pandemic show that people who are significantly overweight or diabetic are much more likely to die from Covid. Also, some scientists have suggested that the Covid vaccine might not offer the same degree of protection if you are overweight.

There is good reason to be fit and healthy.

I talked to Dr Clare Bailey about this. She has been a GP in England for 30 years, and over the years her advice has changed from handing out the same diet sheet to all patients to realising, mainly through the work of her husband Dr Michael Mosley (author of *The Fast Diet* and *The Fast 800 Diet*, which work to help people overcome diabetes), that one diet does not suit all.

She says that when working with patients she tries not to talk about weight in terms of how people look, but more in terms of having a body that functions well so you feel good and you have the nutrition you need to keep your mood and immunity up.

'It's not about having a beach body,' she told me.

When people store their weight around their middle and perhaps around the neck, that means fat is being stored around internal organs, which has a very strong association with a high risk of type 2 diabetes.

In New Zealand there are more than 250,000 people with diabetes (mostly type 2), and the number of people getting diagnosed is rising rapidly.

Clare says that people at high risk respond well to a lower sugar, lower starch and lower calorie approach. But not all healthy eating plans work for all people.

She suggested an experiment she calls the string test: take a piece of string and cut it to your height, then fold it in half. Put the half around your waist — if the ends don't meet then you may have significant risk of type 2 diabetes.

Clare left me with some sage advice.

'It really all comes back to a really simple principle. Give your gut what it needs and it will look after you.'

IN THE YEAR following our first lockdown I decided to do something about how I was looking after my body. Quite simply, to care for it as I would care for my children, my partner, my dad or my pets. I wanted to give it a much higher status than I had previously, which was basically just take what I feed you and keep going, if you don't mind.

I was taking medication for high blood pressure, which previously I had reasoned was genetic. I wasn't sleeping very well. I was carrying extra weight and worrying that it could tip me into type 2 diabetes, which my mother had for half her life. I really didn't want this to happen, having watched her inject herself with insulin several times a day, sometimes even at the dinner table. I would not be that person.

Food

One diet does not fit all. In the past two years or so doctors and scientists have been releasing study after study that proves our food requirements differ widely. Putting the entire population of New Zealand on one eating plan, as advised by health officials for decades, does not work.

This should come as a relief to people who struggle to lose weight or to put it on. Why in one family can you all eat exactly the same thing yet some are small and others are large?

The author of *Spoon-Fed: Why almost everything we've been told about food is wrong*, Tim Spector, knows how to analyse science and discovered to his horror the scandalous lack of good science behind many medical and government food regulations.

I have been a fan of Tim's ever since he wrote *The Diet Myth* back in 2015, when he was one of the first people to talk about gut microbiomes and the need to eat a steak once a month instead of resorting to vitamin B12 injections. We talked one evening on Zoom and I wasn't at all surprised to see a very healthy, fit man my age dressed in a T-shirt, happy to have a chat and a laugh. He has a great sense of humour and obviously cares about his body.

I eagerly read *Spoon-Fed* and before I knew it I was testing my blood glucose levels using the device my mother used to use to control her diabetes. She died in 2019 but my father had tucked it away in the medicine drawer.

The device is a small unit about the size of a credit card; it comes with insertable test strips and a nifty little pencil with a sharp lancet in it. You prime the lancet, then press a button and it attacks your finger enough to produce a drop of blood. The first time I did this, the setting was calibrated quite high for my mother and my finger wouldn't stop bleeding, but I soon got the hang of it. You put some blood on the end of the test strip and the unit will give you a reading.

The theory is you take a blood sugar reading before you eat. For a normal non-diabetic person the reading should fall somewhere between 4 mmol/L and 5.4 mmol/L. This measurement is the number of millimoles (mmol) of glucose per litre (L) of your blood. A millimole is a standard unit for measuring the mass of molecules.

You then test again two hours after a meal to see what has happened to your blood glucose level. At this point it should be no higher than 7.8 mmol/L.

I had to google all this information because even though I'd watched my mother do these tests many times a day for 40 years, I hadn't really paid attention — except to hear when she had a very high reading, which meant things were not good.

The first test I did was before my normal breakfast of toast and tea. Before the meal my reading was 5.1, and two hours after it was 10.5.

I totally freaked out. I am not prone to hypochondria but since my mother's death I had become super-aware that I too could succumb to the myriad of problems her body coped with every day. All I could see was my overweight mother injecting needles into her stomach and constantly monitoring herself every few hours.

'I will not turn out like my mother!' I told my daughter. Not for the first time, to be honest.

I decided that I was pre-diabetic and things needed to change, immediately.

I also started obsessively recording my blood pressure, using my mother's old blood pressure cuff and monitor. I might have been completely freaked out that I was inheriting my mother's medical problems but I was obviously quite okay with using her medical equipment.

I was thinking about my blood pressure because my 89-year-old father had just come off his blood-pressure pills because he was so healthy. He takes no medication and is an inspiration for me.

I kept testing for two weeks and started changing what I was eating based on Tim Spector's observations that carbs can sometimes cause blood sugar spikes. The day I stopped eating processed carbohydrates like bread, pasta and white rice, which were a large part of my diet, my blood sugar readings returned to normal.

About two months later when my doctor was checking my skin for moles, I told her I'd decided I was pre-diabetic. She was mildly horrified, and while she said the no carbs thing was fine, she felt my pre-diabetes diagnosis was a bit of a leap.

'How about we run a blood test and see what's going on?' she said, after gently explaining that one of my moles looked dodgy and would need to be cut out.

There are amazing blood tests for diabetes that track back three months to see if there were any problems. There weren't. I wasn't pre-diabetic.

But by then I had become quite used to not eating processed carbs and I noticed something else. Digestive issues that had plagued me all my life had calmed down. I had lost some weight and was feeling a lot better. My blood pressure had come down significantly.

Tim has found that we aren't all the same when it comes to what causes spikes in our blood glucose levels, which is why one diet won't work for everyone. Some people get massive blood sugar spikes from eating bread, others don't. When you get a spike it means you are putting stress on your pancreas and liver, and those spikes also affect how you process fats and can set up inflammation in your body.

Tim says that the way we eat is often formed in our childhood, such as being told that eating breakfast is the most important meal of the day, eating fish will make you brainy, or having morning and afternoon tea with a biscuit is something you must do. My mother was a big one for insisting on snacking otherwise you would faint. I've never fainted in my life but I was never allowed out of the house without having had something to eat. An empty stomach was my mother's enemy.

'I think it's time to free ourselves from convention and to experiment to see what our body needs and what's good for it,' says Tim. 'We have so much choice and so many ways to experiment and look at different eating patterns.'

Not everyone has a dead diabetic mother's blood sugar monitor they can use, but if you are worried about it you can always buy one for about $30 plus lancets and test strips. Continuous blood sugar monitors are also available, which give a continuous read-out of your blood glucose levels via a patch on your arm, sending data to your smartphone or a monitor. I am keen to try one of these out because who knows what other foods are causing me inflammation, but they are expensive. It also seems a bit dramatic to be that involved in my blood glucose levels, but I think I might just give it a go one day.

Have I just encouraged you to totally freak out and diagnose yourself as pre-diabetic too? I hope not and I'm sorry if I have. But I do think that we are entering an age when monitoring how our body reacts to what we feed it is a good idea. Tim believes that in the future we will all walk around with a monitor of some type attached to us, giving us readings on our smartphones. But for now I don't see anything wrong with seeing what raises our blood sugar and avoiding it.

Tim questions every diet plan, government recommendation, miracle cure or food label and encourages us to think for ourselves rather than go with the flow.

'What I'm trying to do here is give people the wake-up call and tell them they are sleep-walking towards more ill health and obesity if they carry on like this. Don't be a sucker for marketing, don't put up with it. At least have your eyes open and experiment without following some religious dogma because there is no perfect diet out there,' he says.

Myths Tim has busted include the idea that saturated fat is a major cause of heart disease and the one that declares that sugar-free foods are a safe way to lose weight. His advice for eating is simple. Diversity is important and he would like us to eat 20 to 30 different species of plants a week to get a wide range of nutrients.

At first I thought this was impossible, but then I realised that in one meal of salad or stir-fry I could pack in five or six different vegetables, and then there was tofu, baked beans and herbs, plus different fruits and berries as snacks. The following recipes are good examples: my 'Forest muesli' has nine different nuts, fruits and seeds in it, and my 'Easy cabbage salad' features a mixture of sprouted seeds. In reality, 30 different plants in a week is quite doable.

Forest muesli

———

150 g each of four different raw nuts, whole
(I use almonds, walnuts, pistachios and peanuts)

150 g each of three different seeds
(I use pumpkin, sunflower and hemp)

100 g coconut threads or flakes

100 g flax seeds

1 cup dried fruit, chopped (optional)

Heat the oven to 180°C. Spread the nuts on a tray and roast for 5–10 minutes. Keep a close eye on them so they don't burn, and give them a good stir halfway through.

Meanwhile, heat a frying pan over medium heat. Put the seeds in the pan and stir often to 'wake them up'. You want them to heat through but not burn, so keep a close eye on them too.

Let the nuts and seeds cool, then mix with the coconut and flax seeds. You can also add some dried fruit if you like.

Store in an airtight container for up to 4 weeks.

Easy cabbage salad

This is called 'That cabbage salad' in my house.

½ cabbage, finely sliced

1 handful freshly grown sprouts (I like the organic
sweet and spicy mix from kingsseeds.co.nz)

1 tbsp Kewpie mayonnaise

juice of ½ a lemon

salt and pepper, to season

Mix well to create the most divine salad that goes with anything. If
you have any left over, sprinkle it over peanut butter on Vogel's toast in
the morning.

Tim also recommends getting rid of processed foods, not counting calories and feeding your gut with fermented foods.

'Whatever you do, keep your gut microbiome safe. Try the keto diet by all means, but make sure you still eat lots of different plants and go in with your eyes open. Just because it worked for someone you know, doesn't mean it is right for your body.'

I now follow a low-carb diet — well, a version of it. I have cut out processed carbs, which means if it's not on my plate roughly in the form it was grown, then I don't eat it. Bread, pasta and noodles are full of processed white flour, and white rice has had all that valuable fibre and nutrition stripped off it. I also stopped drinking as much alcohol. Slowly but surely my waist got smaller.

At the time I didn't realise that there are about 10 low-carb diets out there, such as Clean Keto, Dirty Keto and Vegan Keto. I just cut out processed carbs, opting to get them from the vegetables I ate far more of every day, and I graciously allowed myself two slices of homemade bread a day just so I knew I wasn't being ridiculous.

I didn't count calories (I could feel my mother turning in her grave) because another thing Tim found out is that not all calories are equal. To be honest, having grown up in a diet-focused household I knew the language of calories just as a child growing up in a bilingual household learns two languages. I found it quite hard to not look at a piece of food and immediately know its calorie content because I had been doing it, along with my mother, all my childhood. It took a while to ignore that language, but I did look at portion size and second helpings.

I wasn't really trying to lose weight; I was trying to avoid my mother's diabetes. I was trying to get those blood sugar readings down to reduce the spikes, which in turn cause inflammation, change the way fats are processed and increase my blood pressure. But I did lose weight — though I can't tell you how much because I haven't weighed myself in decades. And I'm not particularly interested in a headline screaming 'Wendyl's miracle weight loss, her secrets revealed', telling other women statements like 'I lost 20 kg, look at me!' complete with before and after photos.

Like many women I found I had given those scales far too much power in my life. I was not going to be told by my bathroom scales what kind of day I would have depending on whether I had lost or gained a few grams. I had grown up in a house where I had seen my mother get on those scales with absolute fear and trepidation, and often burst into tears. Why would I let those agents of evil live in my bathroom?

But I did measure my waist and saw the centimetres disappear one by one, quite quickly. Soon I had lost 10 centimetres. I visited my doctor, who took my blood pressure and took me off one of my blood-pressure medications. A year later I had lost a total of 20 centimetres. So maybe my high blood pressure was genetic, or maybe it was because I was carrying extra weight. Either way I'm just glad to be off one of those medications.

If you are overweight, losing weight is a healthy decision no matter which way you slice it in the world of body positivity. If you take medication for things like high blood pressure or other health issues like high cholesterol or diabetes, your body is struggling. If you are a large woman whose body is functioning brilliantly on all levels then don't lose weight and please be happy with yourself.

We all know that the BMI measurement, which doctors have traditionally used to work out if you are obese, is ridiculous because it is designed for one body type that the medical profession decided was a standard. Women come in many shapes and sizes and can be perfectly healthy at any size, but if you know that your body could be free of medication if you changed your diet and helped it function as it wants to function then I think it's a good idea to give it a go.

As my doctor told me when she finally cut out the melanoma on my leg, knowing that if she kept talking I would be less likely to cry from the imagined pain I wasn't feeling thanks to a local anaesthetic, 'Women our age just don't need refined carbohydrates any more. We're just not that active.'

She's right. We're no longer running around after children or racing home from work to feed them and do the laundry and read a bedtime story. I know there are women in their late fifties who run marathons, but mostly we're a lot less active at this age and what carbs we do need can come from nuts, seeds and veggies.

Months later my other doctor agreed with my first doctor, but added 'Don't avoid whole-food carbs like beans and lentils. They do give you carbohydrates but new studies are showing that because of their high fibre they don't act like carbs in your system.'

I had been craving baked beans, but when I looked at the ingredients on the tin I realised I was actually just having some beans with my sugar. So I invented my 'Five-minute not-baked beans' (see the next page), which are my go-to meal when I can't be bothered cooking much and might turn to takeaways instead.

I have enjoyed experimenting with a range of beans, from pinto and kidney to black beans. They all have different flavours and I am amazed that while I can appreciate the subtle difference in flavour between different meats, I never knew that beans could provide the same variety. And gradually, thanks to the beans, eggs, tofu and halloumi, I stopped eating so much meat.

Five-minute not-baked beans

*This dish is so simple and so good for you. Serve this
with a fried egg on top or some kimchi.*

400 g can cannellini beans

400 g can chopped tomatoes

1 tbsp Worcestershire sauce

salt and pepper, to taste

2 tbsp grated Parmesan (or more)

1 tbsp chopped fresh herbs — basil is best but
parsley or mint will do in the winter

Drain the beans, then add them to a saucepan with the tomatoes.
Add the Worcestershire sauce and bring to the boil. Taste for salt and
pepper and add if necessary.

Pour into serving bowls, then top with the Parmesan and chopped
herbs. Serve immediately.

Real bean casserole

Sometimes it's nice to have beans slow-cooked — the flavour is amazing. This is my favourite recipe, which I mix up by using different beans. There are so many interesting dried beans out there to try: pinto, black beans, kidney beans, borlotti and more.

I find it crazy that while I know how different cuts of meat taste, I had no idea that beans had such amazingly diverse flavours. When I first made this with pinto beans I couldn't believe how meaty the broth tasted when no meat had been added. I also like that you don't add any stock; the flavour is mostly from the beans.

My favourite beans for this recipe are pinto or black beans. You can leave out the bacon for a vegetarian version. Be aware that the different types of beans all have different cooking times.

400 g dried beans	3 tbsp olive oil
2 cloves garlic	400 g spinach or silverbeet
1 small piece dried chilli	salt and pepper, to season
salt	8 slices of bacon

Cover the beans in water and leave to soak for 12 hours — I usually do this when I go to bed and leave overnight.

Drain the beans and put in a nice big pot, preferably with a heavy bottom. Cover with 2 litres of water and add the garlic, chilli, a pinch of salt and the olive oil.

Bring to the boil, then reduce the heat and leave to cook, covered, for as long as it takes to cook the beans you have chosen. (See guide at the end of this recipe.) Make sure there is always a couple of centimetres of water above the beans by topping up with boiling water as you need to.

About 15 minutes before your beans are cooked, add the thinly cut silverbeet or spinach, stems included. When it is wilted down — about 15 minutes — taste for salt and pepper and add if necessary.

Cut your bacon into small pieces and fry, then add to the stew. Pour in an extra glug of olive oil, then serve. I sometimes add a poached egg on top as well.

Bean cooking times

This is just a guide. When beans are cooked they should be soft, almost melt-in-the-mouth, so keep cooking for a little longer if you haven't achieved this in the time given below.

Black turtle: 50–60 minutes

Borlotti: 60–90 minutes

Cannellini: 90–120 minutes

Kidney: 70–90 minutes

Fava (broad) beans: 50–70 minutes

Pinto: 90 minutes

White/haricot beans: 45–60 minutes

I NOW KNOW that for my body, processed carbs are not king. In fact I just don't need them to be healthy.

According to a *Guardian* story, 'Legumes are one of the most nutrient-rich crops on the market — they are abundant in protein, fibre, iron and potassium — and they are a healthier alternative to cereals and meat.'

The article goes on to say that eating legumes is not only good for us but also good for the planet: 'While traditional European crops such as oats, barley, wheat and rapeseed require synthetic fertilisers to obtain nitrogen — a critical nutrient for growth — leguminous plants produce their own nitrogen from the air. They also leave nitrogen behind in the soil, ready to be used by future crops.'

So eating beans is actually a good environmental decision as well, because you're encouraging more farmers to grow legumes and not use synthetic fertilisers.

As always, there's a caveat — do be aware that for some people carbs are essential. We are all different.

And while we're at it, let's talk about prescriptive eating. Just because you're trying something new like low carbs, it doesn't mean it should take over your life.

If I'm at a restaurant, which is a rare thing these days because we live in the Hokianga, I will treasure that meal and order exactly what I feel like. That freshly baked bread becomes a positive food memory for me that I cherish.

Every Saturday I make a loaf of bread — we eat some of it and Dad gets the rest. Saturdays are my day for carbs and I love it.

One Sunday night Paul took me to an Auckland Wagner Society event featuring renowned Kiwi tenor Simon O'Neill. Paul is into Wagner and I am slowly being indoctrinated, although it will be a cold day in Valhalla when I sit through all 14 hours of the Ring Cycle over four days. There was a break for tea, and sitting on the cake table was the most delicious date slice that one of the Wagner ladies had made. I had five pieces and two cups of tea and dreamed about it for days. Positive food memories are important!

Tim Spector's 12-point plan

1. Eat diverse foods, mainly plants, without added chemicals.

2. Question the science and don't believe quick-fix, single solutions.

3. Don't be fooled by labels or marketing.

4. Understand that you are not average when it comes to food.

5. Don't get into food ruts: diversify and experiment.

6. Experiment with meal timings and skipping meals.

7. Use real food, not supplements.

8. Avoid ultra-processed foods with over ten ingredients.

9. Eat foods to improve gut microbe diversity.

10. Reduce regular blood glucose and blood fat spikes.

11. Reduce meat and fish consumption and check its sustainability.

12. Educate yourself and the next generation in the importance of real food.

If you're reading this book then you are probably good at reading the labels on your food at the supermarket. Most of us have learned to decipher these labels and check that there's not too much sugar or chemicals in what we are eating. But is that enough?

Endocrinologist Robert Lustig says no, and he should know because he's been studying processed food for decades and established the anti-sugar movement with his YouTube lecture *Sugar: The bitter truth*. I've interviewed him a couple of times over the years and he is determined to expose the wrongdoings of the food industry, particularly for over-engineering our food to the point where it damages our health.

His latest book, *Metabolical: The truth about processed food and how it poisons people and the planet*, could win awards for having the longest title ever. In it, he points out that even healthy-sounding food like hummus or sushi can be so processed that it has been stripped of its beneficial properties and sprinkled with toxins that stress the liver and the gut.

He wants us to eat 'real' food — nothing processed that comes in a pot, even if it looks like the hummus you make at home. On this we are aligned, as my healthy eating message for years has been to 'eat like your nana', and is based on what my nana would have been eating in the early 1900s when there was no such thing as processed food. Everything you ate came in its natural state unless it was baked, and even then it didn't have additives to make it rise quicker or last longer.

Robert won't give you any points for bothering to read the labels of your supermarket food because he says they just tell you what is *in* the food, not what has been *done* to the food. He argues that 70 per cent of the items in United States supermarkets are ultra-processed, which means that most of the food eaten in the States is not real.

A quick look around your local supermarket will tell you that the outside ring of the supermarket is where you will find food in the form

it was intended, such as whole vegetables and fruit, meat and fish, most milk and free-range eggs. The rest is processed in some way.

The main reason food began to be processed five decades ago was to make it last. Micronutrients turn rancid when exposed to oxygen, so food wasn't able to sit on the shelf for long.

Then came the idea that adding stuff to real food was a good idea. That way manufacturers could change food's flavour, colour, texture and shelf life. I used to write extensively about food additives for my column 'Wendyl Wants to Know' in *The New Zealand Herald* so I won't bore you with it all again, but let's just take a look at one additive that is in most processed food. Sugar.

Sugar is added to processed food to add bulk, to give it a lovely caramel colour, to help maintain moisture on the shelf and to preserve it.

While writing my column for the *Herald*, I became very distrustful of all supermarket food, and that sparked my interest in growing my own vegetables, making my own bread, roasting my own coffee beans, using tea leaves and a teapot, keeping chickens for eggs, eating homekill beef, not eating farmed fish, making my own yoghurt and buying only organic, non-homogenised and if possible non-pasteurised milk — preferably from the farm gate — and cheese from proper cheese shops or delis where the provenance is printed on it.

And even though I do all this, I have no idea what happened to my tea leaves, coffee or flour before I bought them, but I kid myself that buying organic means they're hopefully pretty clean.

It used to feel a bit mad, but now it's normal for me. I don't eat any processed food unless my granddaughters are around, and much to their parents' horror we buy them sweets and I eat a few just for fun. And of course if I'm at someone's house and they've prepared a meal for me, I will always eat it no matter where it came from. That's just polite.

Meat-free meals

A lot of people are cutting down on the amount of meat they eat for various reasons. My reason is simply that I like to add more variety to my diet, and I do this by eating more legumes and vegetables.

I am also leaning away from heavy meals every night, even though Paul loves them. A big chunk of meat with a few vegetables just doesn't appeal to me, especially in the summer. Here are some meals I make often, sometimes just for me, and Paul will have them as a side dish to some sausages or steak. The important thing is that they are delicious and easy to prepare.

A great base salad

To make a great salad you need a variety of greens to give you a mix of flavours. Here's a simple base for the following salads.

If you are using bagged salad leaves, pick one with lots of different varieties in it like mesclun and maybe add a bag of rocket to spice it up a bit. Always, and I mean always, empty the leaves into a bowl of cold water and leave them to soak. A couple of hours is great but even 10 minutes makes a difference to their crispness and flavour, and you'll have rinsed off anything that was put in that bag to keep them fresh. If you are picking salad leaves from your garden, soak them in water for 10 minutes anyway so that dirt falls to the bottom and any bugs float to the top.

Lay out a clean tea towel, then drain your salad leaves and lay them out all over your tea towel. If it's from my garden I like to inspect each leaf in case there is an insect that needs to be relocated after its bath.

Gently roll up the tea towel and press the water out of your leaves. Unroll and take what you need. If there is any left over, roll the tea towel up again and put it in the fridge. Your leaves will last a good few days like this.

Dress your salad with a swig of good-quality cold-pressed olive oil followed by a swig of balsamic vinegar. I use a beautiful pomegranate balsamic vinegar I buy online from Divinity Olives.

Gently mix the dressing into your salad with your hands to get each leaf coated deliciously.

Beetroot, feta and walnut salad

My kids love it when I make this on my trips to Auckland. It is so easy to put together. If you can source the pomegranate balsamic it is worth it because the flavour blends so well with the sweetness of the beetroot.

base salad (see page 122, but hold the dressing)

4 large cooked beetroot or 6–8 small ones (you can cook them yourself but if you're in a hurry you can buy precooked vacuum-packed beetroot in the vegetable section of your supermarket)

200 g packet feta

1 cup raw walnuts

juice of 1 lemon

pomegranate balsamic vinegar or plain balsamic vinegar

good-quality cold-pressed olive oil

sea salt and pepper, to season

Spread out the base salad on a large serving platter. Dry the feta between some paper towels then cut into 1 cm cubes and sprinkle over the salad.

Chop the beetroot into similar-size pieces as the feta and sprinkle it over the base salad.

Chop the walnuts into small pieces and gently dry-fry until they are just starting to brown. Sprinkle these on top of everything else.

Squeeze over the lemon juice, then drizzle liberally with pomegranate balsamic or balsamic vinegar, then olive oil. Finish with a healthy sprinkling of sea salt and pepper.

Tofu salad

This is a great quick salad, especially if you have your salad greens wrapped up in your tea towel in the fridge ready to go.

300 g packet firm tofu

2 tsp salt

½ cup cornflour

1 tsp onion powder

olive oil for frying

base salad (see page 122)

handful cherry tomatoes, chopped in half

Take the tofu out of its packet and wrap it in a clean tea towel. Place on a board and put a weight on it for at least half an hour, or preferably an hour. I use a loaf tin with a couple of cans of tomatoes in it as a weight. This gets all the moisture out, which helps the tofu crisp up in the pan. Genius.

Cut the tofu into small rectangles or cubes and sprinkle with 1 teaspoon salt. Roll the tofu around in it.

Put the cornflour, the remaining salt and the onion powder in a bowl. Mix together and then toss the tofu in this mixture.

Cover the bottom of a solid-based frying pan with olive oil and heat until hot. Cook the tofu in batches, turning to ensure each side gets golden brown. This should take about 10 minutes.

When it is all cooked give it a final sprinkle of salt and pepper and throw it into your base salad along with the tomatoes. I don't usually dress this salad, but sometimes I sprinkle over my homemade tomato sauce (see page 127) or Paul's sweet chilli sauce (see page 130), or give it a squirt of mayonnaise.

Halloumi salad

200 g packet halloumi

olive oil for frying

1 red capsicum

1 cup mushrooms

base salad (see page 122)

Take your halloumi out of the packet and soak it in cold water for half an hour to reduce the salt. Skip this step if you like your halloumi salty.

Remove the moisture from the halloumi as for the tofu in the tofu salad recipe (page 124). Cut the halloumi into pieces.

Heat olive oil in a solid-based frying pan and fry halloumi until golden brown. This doesn't take long. Test to see that the pieces of halloumi are soft and molten in the middle.

Meanwhile cut up the capsicum and mushrooms. In another pan, gently fry until the mushrooms are soft and fragrant and the capsicum is just starting to brown.

Toss the capsicum and mushrooms into your base salad followed by the cooked halloumi.

I don't usually dress this salad, but feel free to add my tomato sauce (see page 127), Paul's sweet chilli sauce (see page 130), mayonnaise or your favourite dressing or sauce.

Pumpkin cashew curry

---

*This recipe was inspired by my friend Nici Wickes, the
amazing and inspiring food writer. I love a good curry using
vegetables and this one fits the bill on any night.*

4 tbsp olive oil

2 tsp mustard seeds

1 tsp cumin seeds

1 tsp turmeric

1 large onion, thinly sliced

500 g pumpkin, peeled
and cubed to bite size

½ cup raw cashews

2 tbsp fresh grated ginger

½ tsp brown sugar

400 ml can coconut milk

juice of 1 lemon

salt and pepper, to season

In a large pan, heat the oil and fry the mustard seeds until they start to
pop. Add the cumin, turmeric and onion, then sauté for 15 minutes or
until the onion has browned.

Add the pumpkin, cashews and ginger, then sprinkle over the sugar.
Fry, without stirring, until some nuts and pieces of pumpkin are
golden.

Pour in the coconut milk, then cover and simmer for approximately
15 minutes until the pumpkin is tender. Squeeze in the lemon juice
and season with salt and pepper.

Tomato sauce

I have made hundreds of bottles of tomato sauce in my life and none of them really did the trick until I found a recipe by my friend Nici Wickes and adapted that. I think the secret is her addition of a can of tomatoes, which seems a bit counterintuitive when you are trying to use up your haul of fresh tomatoes, but I think it really adds colour and flavour. Nici is always right when it comes to great recipes! I also like that you don't have to fart around peeling tomatoes and all that nonsense. This recipe makes about 2 litres.

2 kg fresh tomatoes, roughly chopped

400 g can crushed tomatoes

2 large apples, roughly chopped

2 large onions, roughly chopped

1 cup brown sugar

1 cup raw sugar

1 cup malt vinegar

2 cups apple cider vinegar

2 tbsp salt

1 tsp black pepper

1 tsp ground allspice

½ tsp ground cloves

Bring all the ingredients to the boil in a large pot and simmer vigorously for about 2 hours until the sauce is completely pulpy — it ought to have thickened a bit by then too.

In batches, put it through a blender until smooth. Don't over-blend as that will lighten the colour to orange.

Sterilise bottles or jars by heating them in an oven at 100°C for 15 minutes. Pour the hot sauce into the bottles or jars and seal with lids. Wipe clean and allow to cool.

Paul's sweet chilli sauce

Every year I grow a couple of chilli plants — some years they are very quiet and just give us a few chillies, but one year we had hundreds. To use them up, Paul created this recipe, which is loved by all our family. When we have a bad chilli year he resorts to buying chillies just to keep the kids supplied with their bottles of chilli sauce.

20 red chillies, whole

5 cm piece ginger, peeled, roughly chopped

8 cloves garlic, peeled

2 cups sugar

2 cups white vinegar

2 tbsp fish sauce

Place the chillies, ginger and garlic in the bowl of a small food processor and process until finely chopped.

Place the sugar and vinegar in a saucepan over a low heat and stir without boiling until the sugar has dissolved.

Add the chilli, garlic and ginger paste to the sugar syrup and simmer for 25–30 minutes, until thickened. Add the fish sauce and simmer for a further 1–2 minutes. Pour into sterilised bottles (see page 127) and when cool store in the refrigerator for up to 6 months.

Cashew salsa

This salsa goes so well with curries, but is also delicious sprinkled on a bowl of hot noodles or rice. This recipe is written in my recipe book in a very vague and haphazard way without any measurements, so I'm wondering if I persuaded someone to write it in at a dinner party one night after a few wines! I've figured out some measurements that work for me.

1 cup raw cashews

½ cup shredded or desiccated coconut

3 makrut (kaffir) lime leaves, shredded, or zest of 1 lime (you can leave the lime leaves out if you don't have them but it is much nicer with them)

1 chilli, finely chopped (without seeds if you don't like it hot)

2 tbsp chopped coriander

1 lime (or lemon if you don't have lime)

1 tsp sweet chilli sauce

1 tsp fish sauce

½ tsp brown sugar

Toast the cashews in a frying pan until they are just starting to brown. Throw them in a mortar and pestle and add the coconut, lime leaves or zest, chilli and coriander. Bash away until they are all combined and mushy — you still want chunks so don't get carried away.

Squeeze the lime or lemon over the mixture, then add the sweet chilli sauce, fish sauce and brown sugar. Stir it all together and serve. I just leave it all in the mortar and pestle.

Body talk

Part of caring for your body includes not trash-talking it. Why would you be so mean to something that is so important when it comes to keeping you alive and well?

Isn't it amazing how much time we spend thinking about our bodies? Too fat, too thin, too floppy, too bulgy. Or is it just me? I don't know because all I've ever known since I was a little girl was that bodies were made to be criticised and judged. My mother stood in judgement of every single body she ever met and vocalised her judgement the minute that poor body's back was turned. Was this unusual? I don't think it was, judging by the number of people who have sent me messages every time I write about this.

So I'm going to presume that you, as you're reading this, are nodding in agreement and sighing along with me, and are eager to see if something can be done about this terrible state of affairs. If not, feel free to skip this bit and I send you off with a sincere pat on the back and well done you, or in some cases lucky you for being brought up in an environment where what you are is good enough. Off you go . . .

But back to bodies and how to be at peace with yours. You might think you could get rid of all your mirrors, and live in isolation where you never see anyone and the look on their face when they judge you, and be very happy. But you wouldn't be happy because we are all worth looking at in the mirror and thousands of studies prove that being connected to other people is vitally important for our mental health.

Here are some things I have found useful in my quest to stop judging my body shape. I feel that if we can learn to live with ourselves we can then move on to other fun things like building our immunity, ocean swimming, sleeping more and drinking less.

Ask yourself what evidence you have that your arms are ugly

Not so long ago, I was overworked and grumpy and thinking of resigning from all my work and hiding away in my house in the Hokianga where I would get really serious about growing all my vegetables to eat because we would have no money due to the resigning from all my work.

At the time it seemed like quite a good idea but then I got on a Zoom call with the fabulous food writer Nici Wickes, who used to live next door to me years ago (and put up with our teenagers having wild parties when we went away). She also put together fabulous food pages for my magazine *Thrive*. We had been emailing about what she would do for the next issue and realised we were both a bit grumpy. So Nici suggested a cheer-up Zoom, to which I grumpily agreed.

The next thing I knew we were looking at each other on our computers and I had to laugh at how similar we looked. Neither of us had brushed our hair, we had not put any make-up on and we were both wearing similar baggy, possibly not that clean (well, mine wasn't), black-and-white-striped T-shirts. We could have been twins.

Nici reached out to me that day and I was so grateful. At that stage we were not close friends, but knew and liked and respected each other.

She got me talking about what was going on, and I shared with her something that had just happened to me. I had arrived home back up north after spending three weeks in Auckland working on the launch of my new magazine. Before I left the Hokianga I had spent six months carefully seeding wildflowers into my orchard. It was a labour of love that involved raising them from seeds on my sundeck then transplanting them carefully into the orchard then covering them so that the chickens wouldn't dig them up.

Just before I left they were finally taking shape and I was looking forward to sitting on my orchard seat on a sunny afternoon watching my wildflowers gently sway in the breeze, knowing that they were benefiting all sorts of insects and bees while being so beautiful.

But in my absence weeds grew. I love weeds and try to work with them as much as possible, but these weeds — mainly dock weed — had grown over a metre tall and were essentially blocking any light from getting on to my precious juvenile flowers.

So I asked the guy who helps us with odd jobs to cut the weeds down a bit.

'Not too much, just so that the wildflowers can get light and get some growth,' I said. I even indicated with my hands how much, about 30 centimetres.

Then I went away for the day.

I arrived back to find that in my absence the god of scorched earth had moved in and removed every living flower and weed from the land beneath the trees in my orchard. It was barren and bereft.

I stood in the middle of it and burst into a flood of tears. They streamed out of my eyes and would not stop.

I was a little surprised, as I'm not prone to bursting into tears. So I stood there and wiped my eyes and realised that I wasn't crying about the wildflowers. I could plant more, that is the beauty of gardening. Things grow back. What I was doing was releasing stress. The past three weeks had been hard. Enjoyable but hard and I was carrying some stuff that was worrying me.

So I went for a walk on the beach with the dogs and set about sorting it all out.

I realised that 95 per cent of what I do in life — work and pleasure — is sheer joy. I love it. The other 5 per cent is annoying and I worry about that, but it's also something I can't change. I can't change the way people do things that annoy me. I can't change the way stuff happens in life.

So I decided that instead of letting 5 per cent of stuff I can't change take over 95 per cent of my thoughts and emotions, I would simply dismiss that 5 per cent and throw it away, recognising it as a waste of space in my head.

And so the 5 per cent rule was born. I decided that if something happens that I can't change, I name it as part of the 5 per cent and banish it from my head.

Nici listened to me and then shared what was going on with her life, which involved taking her laptop outside to show me her new pool — one of those pop-up ones. It was the middle of summer and she was bathing in it several times a day.

'Get one — you'll love it,' she shouted enthusiastically.

She also talked about her love of ocean swimming, which I related to far more than the swimming pool. Little did I know then that two weeks after that chat I would start ocean swimming — and I haven't stopped yet.

Nici also shared some podcasts that had helped her, and one sounded like just what I needed. It featured the former Chief Business Officer for Google and author of *Solve for Happy*, Mo Gawdat. He wrote his book after his son died while undergoing a standard surgical procedure and he decided to retrain his brain from having negative thoughts.

The thing Nici and I both took from it is that when your brain gives you negative thoughts, which most brains do, you need to stand up to it and say this simple thing: 'What evidence do you have for that?' We can change the way our brain talks to us just by standing up to those thoughts instead of calmly accepting them. After a while your brain gets retrained into not doing it any more.

Mo has given his negative brain a name, but I've been more accepting of negative Wendyl because she is, after all, part of me and who I am.

My first conversation with my negative brain came the next day when I was standing in front of the mirror — a common meeting place with your negative brain. I was wearing a sleeveless dress and my negative brain told me that my 58-year-old arms were disgusting. They were crêpe-y and flabby and should be hidden from sight. I realised, and wasn't at all surprised, that my negative brain talked a lot like my mother used to.

So I stood there and said 'What evidence do you have for that?' The answer came back in my mother's voice, saying 'Women shouldn't show parts of their body that aren't perfect.' Wow. It then continued to repeat a story a friend of mine tells about one of her teachers, whose flabby arms would erase the chalk on the board while she was writing on it. *Ha.* I countered with the statement that I have never looked at a woman's arms and thought she should hide them away. Well, not recently anyway. And that a woman should be free to choose not to wear sleeves on a hot summer's day. And that all I think when I see a woman in a sleeveless dress or top is how cool and comfortable she must be.

This conversation was silent, as I was talking to myself in my head, but it took a good five minutes. Then I kept the dress on and went out for the day. Perhaps someone judged my arms, but I didn't notice.

That's the secret. First deal with your own negativity and then put up a shield against negativity from others. There is a saying I use in my head a lot when I'm out and about: 'I don't remember asking for your opinion.' If my negative brain decides to tell me that someone in the room is staring at my horrible arms because I had the effrontery to let them out for the day, I just turn it around and say to my horrible negative brain 'I don't remember asking for your opinion.'

This line is a great comeback whether you say it out loud or just say it to yourself.

Don't set unrealistic body goals

If I'm honest, I will always say that my ideal body is that of a tall, skinny rock chick like Chrissie Hynde or Patti Smith. That's because before I had body issues in my late twenties, I was a tall, skinny girl who wore band T-shirts and skinny jeans and hung out with rock bands. Even if she smoked and drank and took drugs, I want her back. Badly.

But let's look at the word 'ideal' and in particular the synonyms for it. Ideal means perfect. And its synonyms are excellent, exemplary, faultless, model, optimal and optimum.

Are we really going to talk to ourselves about an ideal body? No, because no one is any of those words.

Realistically my body is not going to return to its former self nearly 40 years later. That's not going to happen because I'm not young any more and that isn't who I am any more. I still wear band T-shirts when I'm gardening and skinny jeans — but the stretchy ones.

So recently, and I'm ashamed to say how recently this was (a month ago as I'm writing this), I just let that rock chick go into the past, which is where she belongs, along with her packet of fags, bleached blonde hair and fuck-you attitude. You were cool, Wendyl, but you are blessed and released.

When I started losing weight, Patti Smith and Chrissie Hynde came back into my life. There they were, saying 'Come join us, we're so cool!' Then I realised that as much as I love them both I'm not going to wear my grey hair in two long plaits à la Patti Smith and I'm not really up to wearing as much eyeliner as Chrissie Hynde. It may be cool, but no.

Instead I think I'll settle for whatever my body gives me and that's about it. I really don't care as long as I can get down the paddock to my ocean swim most days, and have a good day in the garden and not ache too much. My body is strong and capable, and that's fine with me.

When in doubt, just don't

We all like to create our own personal style. Usually we base it on someone we admire or on a designer or retail store who makes nice clothes.

This can lead to mishaps, in my experience.

In 2020 I joined the board of Consumer NZ. It had been a very long time since I'd had to dress up in anything resembling a corporate wardrobe. I had thrown all those clothes out and gone a bit feral up north in my comfortable clothes. Leggings, jeans, shorts, T-shirts, jumpers. Lovely.

Then I had my first meeting in Wellington and thought I would buy something on Lambton Quay the day before the meeting. I settled for a skirt that I thought would do the trick. It was bright green satin. I know.

On the day of the meeting I turned up looking like no one I knew.

The meeting was going well when we broke for coffee and tea. I walked confidently across the room and helped myself to a coffee and a delicious-looking cheese scone (I wasn't low carb at the time). I had a coffee in one hand and the scone in the other.

As I walked back to the board table — a distance of about five metres — I felt a strange sensation. My skirt had decided to slowly slip down my hips, then my thighs, then my knees until it triumphantly landed in a heap on the floor around my ankles.

I was standing in the middle of the room wearing just my tights.

Somehow I managed to hobble over to the table, put my mug and plate down and frantically haul up my skirt.

I looked around to see if anyone had seen, and was relieved that no one was staring at the new board member at her first board meeting doing an involuntary striptease in the middle of the room.

Then I looked at my friend and co-board member Sue Kedgley, who smiled and said, rather disbelievingly, 'Did that really just happen?'

It was so awful that I forgot about it until the next day when I told my husband in horror. He thought it was extremely funny and so did I, 24 hours later.

But a lesson was learned.

My body works well in what it is used to. It doesn't like tight jeans that leave red marks around my waist. Nor does it like tight bras that leave marks on my shoulders and around my rib cage.

Instead, it likes clothes that fit, stay put and are not trying too hard.

Microbiome

If you don't know what a microbiome is, you really should. We are slowly realising that your gut microbiome — the bacteria in your gut — affects your health in so many ways. It can cause inflammation in your body, mental health issues, allergies . . . the list goes on.

Readers of my other books will know that I'm a FODMAP diet survivor, which helped me realise that I couldn't digest fructans — basically onions and garlic. So I went off them and other fructan foods for a couple of years and now I can eat them again. The theory behind this is that during those two years my gut settled instead of being inflamed every time I ate onion soup, and slowly my microbiome improved and now is happy to take a little cooked onion or garlic. But not raw. Never raw. Never, ever raw. I am that annoying person who picks all the red onion out of her salad.

There are so many products out there being marketed to help your gut microbiome and you're welcome to try whatever you like. I decided to follow Tim Spector's suggestions and continue eating a really diverse diet of lots of different plant foods.

Then I discovered nuts and seeds. I'd always been told to avoid nuts because they are so high in fat, but guess what? Nuts contain 'good' fat and because of their high fibre content the fat is digested differently in the gut.

I read somewhere, probably on Instagram, where I used to follow a plethora of scientists and doctors working in this field, that because of their high fibre, nuts and seeds act as a forest in your gut, providing safe harbour to good bacteria and also nourishing it.

That image in my head made so much sense. I imagined a lovely forest scene where instead of birds and plants thriving there were millions of friendly, smiling bacteria hanging off the trees.

Then a nutritionist said that fibre in the gut is like weights at the gym. It gives your colon something to lift and shove, which keeps it fit and toned.

That was it. I needed to lift my fibre game. I decided to start my day with my 'Forest muesli' (see page 106). I eat a mere third of a cup of this every morning with a bit of Jersey cow organic milk or almond milk, and homemade yoghurt or coconut yoghurt topped with a bit of fruit, whatever is in season and preferably grown on my property.

Within days of starting this regime my gut settled down and signed off from giving me any issues. I don't even think I fart any more!

After a lifetime of dodgy tummy troubles, including being diagnosed with IBS in my early twenties and never really wanting to be far from a toilet, my life turned around thanks to fibre.

I can now afford to be miles away from a toilet and not even think about it, like normal people. All because of a third of a cup of nuts and seeds. Now when I travel the 'Forest muesli' comes along with me because there is not a day that goes by when I don't feed my forest.

I was pleasantly surprised to work out how much fibre I was consuming in a day. When I reduced processed carbs I replaced pasta, rice and bread with more vegetables on my plate, which increased my fibre intake. I was now eating about 30 g of fibre a day, which is the recommended daily amount. I was finally fibre fit.

Robert Lustig supports this turnaround in my gut health. He says that fibre will transform your gut health. He told *The Times*:

> Most of us don't get enough fibre. Our ancestors ate up to 100g a day of fibre, and while the recommended daily amount in the UK is only 30g, women consume a daily average of just 17.2g and men 20.1g. If you don't eat enough fibre you are effectively allowing the bad bacteria in your gut to thrive, resulting in a rising risk of ill health.
>
> The 100 trillion bacteria in your gut need feeding and fibre fulfils that role, but without it the intestinal bacteria feed on you. They start to chew away at the mucin layer that protects the gut lining so that, eventually, there are holes in the intestinal barrier, causing leaky gut syndrome. If bacteria break through the barrier into the bloodstream, they are carried to the liver, causing inflammation and insulin resistance, both of which are damaging.
>
> Yet my colleagues have shown in trials that you can take a crappy microbiome and turn it into a healthy one in two days by eating more fibre. We should eat more foods that contain it, including wholegrains, nuts and seeds, oats, barley and rye, berries, broccoli and leafy greens. Canned and frozen varieties of fruit and veg are what are termed minimally processed — just avoid any with added sugar.

It is worth doing some research into what else feeds your gut microbiome, and allow it to thrive in your fibre forest. See if you can introduce more good bugs into your life through your food.

Our family has embraced this way of eating — my son makes a mean kombucha and my daughter makes a ridiculously awesome kimchi. I make cider vinegar each year using the same mother, which is now six years old; Paul makes a mean shrub (a cider-vinegar-based thirst quencher); and a friend makes an amazing sourdough. I no longer do because I eat less bread. I make my own yoghurt and sauerkraut, and I keep a jar of really easy-to-make vegetable pickles in the fridge that I dip in and out of, usually teaming them with cheese. You'll find most of these recipes in the next few pages.

The secret to getting good bug food into your gut is that you don't need to eat a lot of it. I used to have a whole cup of sauerkraut on my plate, which quite frankly is a lot of sauerkraut to eat in one serving. You just need a little bit, maybe a tablespoon of yoghurt on your cereal, a small glass of kombucha, or a tablespoon of kimchi with your fried eggs — one of my favourite lunches.

There is also a wealth of good bacteria to be found even in one single apple. An Austrian study found that a typical apple carries more than 100 million bacteria, some of which are important in maintaining a healthy gut microbiome.

Cooking will kill most of them, so the emphasis is on eating raw fruit, organic if you can.

The same study found that organic apples harboured a more diverse and balanced bacterial community than conventionally grown apples. And the fresher they are, the better.

I'm growing two apple trees in my orchard, fully intending to use them as my primary source of fruit bacteria, along with my pears.

Kombucha

*You will need to persuade someone to give you a bit of scoby
from their kombucha for this recipe. You can usually find
helpful people on Facebook, or you can buy it online.*

3 cups water

½ cup sugar

4 teabags

scoby

Boil the water. Remove water from the heat, then add the sugar and
teabags. Leave it all to cool, then remove the teabags and pour into a
large clean glass jar.

Add the scoby and cover the open jar with a tea towel, then leave it
somewhere warm in your kitchen but not in direct sun.

After 10 days to 2 weeks it should be gently fizzy and ready to
taste. Take out your scoby and put it in a new batch of kombucha to
keep the scoby going. Store the kombucha you have just made in the
fridge for up to 2 weeks. You can flavour it with a dash of cordial if
you prefer.

Sauerkraut

---

2 cabbages — one white, one red

2 tbsp fine sea salt (unprocessed, not iodised)

1 tbsp caraway seeds

1 tbsp celery seeds

Finely chop or mandolin the cabbage and put it in a clean bucket, sprinkling with the salt as you go. Sprinkle the seeds over the cabbage and mix it all up really well with your (clean) hands.

Find a plate with a circumference just a little smaller than your bucket and sit it inside the bucket on top of the cabbage. Then find a very heavy weight like a big stone or a jar filled with water. I use the base of my very heavy mortar and pestle.

Cover the bucket with a tea towel and store in a cool, dark place. A basement is perfect, as the cabbage can get a little smelly.

The cabbage should release water and sit under the liquid at all times. Keep an eye on it as you don't want it to dry out. If a little surface growth appears, just scrape it off. It's all part of the fermentation.

The sauerkraut can ferment for 1–3 weeks. Taste it and see if you like it after a week.

Place in sterilised jars (see page 127) with some of the liquid and a tight-fitting lid. Store in the fridge, and if you give it to someone tell them to use it within 3 weeks of opening.

* If you have one of those lovely old stone crockpots with a lid, this is ideal for making sauerkraut.

Kimchi

I love making kimchi because it's so easy and tastes so great.
Some recipes add dried shrimp but I prefer to keep it simple.
You'll find daikon radish in Asian grocery stores, and perhaps in
supermarkets too. I don't make my kimchi very spicy so you might
want to double the amount of chilli flakes if you'd like a kick.

1 green cabbage

½ cup good-quality
salt (not iodised)

about 12 cups water

1 daikon radish, cut into
5 cm matchsticks

4 spring onions, cut into pieces

1 tsp chilli flakes, Korean
if you can find them

¼ cup fish sauce

1 tbsp chopped fresh ginger

1 tbsp finely chopped garlic

1 tsp sugar

Chop the cabbage into 5 cm pieces — use only the leaves, not the root end. Put in a large glass or ceramic bowl, sprinkle with the salt, then use your hands to mix all the salt into the cabbage. Add enough cold water to just cover the cabbage.

Cover with plastic wrap and let sit for 24 hours.

Drain the cabbage in a colander and rinse with cold water.

Squeeze out the liquid from the cabbage and put the cabbage in a bowl.

Put all the remaining ingredients in a large bowl and stir to combine. Add the cabbage and toss with your hands to evenly coat the cabbage.

Pack this into a clean 2-litre glass jar and seal. It is a good idea to use a fermenting lid that lets the gas escape as the kimchi ferments, otherwise you will need to take the lid off every few days.

Put your jar in a dark, cool place for two to three days, then store in the fridge. This will keep in the fridge for a month.

Apple cider vinegar

———————

enough chopped cooking apples to fill a regular-sized bucket

boiling water, cooled

3 cups white sugar

Boil enough water to fill the bucket. Let cool. Wash, chop and roughly process the apples — skins, cores and all — in your food processor. Add the cooled water and the apples to the bucket. Cover with a tea towel or loose lid and stir daily for a week.

At the end of the week, strain and add the sugar to the liquid. Stir to dissolve.

Pour into a clean bucket and leave in a cool cupboard for 2 months. When the 'mother' (a sort of leathery translucent skin) forms on top of the liquid, your cider vinegar is ready to strain. Pour into sterilised bottles (see page 127).

Easy vegetable pickle

---

*All you need to make this is sea salt, good-quality water, vegetables
and some spices. If you're going to commit to making vegetable pickle
regularly then I recommend buying an airlock fermenting jar top, which
is designed to let the gas out so that you don't have to keep burping your
jar. A glass weight is also a good idea to keep the vegetables submerged
in the pickling fluid. You can buy good ones at countrytrading.co.*

*Please use a 500 ml glass jar, not plastic, and make sure
that you have poured some boiling water into it and let it
sit for a while before using to kill off anything yucky.*

Vegetables

These can be whatever you love or have in your garden or were tempted
to buy at the supermarket because they looked delicious. Try to eat
seasonally if you can. In summer I pickle cucumber, peppers, courgette
and cabbage and in winter I turn to carrot, onion, cauliflower and broccoli.

Water

If you can buy filtered water or have rain water because you live in
the country this is the best stuff because it doesn't contain chlorine,
which can kill good bugs. I call it 'good' water. Next time it rains
put a clean bucket outside to collect the rain and use that.

Salt

I like to use sea salt for this but feel free to use other salts
if you like — just make sure it's just salt and hasn't any
additions like iodine. I make my own sea salt in the summer.
You'll need 1 tbsp salt for a 500 ml jar of pickle.

Spice

You can use any combinations you like. I usually have a packet of
Gregg's whole pickling spice on hand and sprinkle some of that in
the jar. It has pimento, peppercorns, cassia, ginger, cloves, coriander
and chilli in it. Sometimes I add celery seed (mainly because I have a
huge jar of it I collected from my garden one summer and it needs to
be used up) and mustard seed. Turmeric will make everything yellow
but won't add a terrific amount of flavour. Good spices to use include
coriander seeds, cumin seeds, black peppercorns, mustard seeds and
chilli flakes. Some people add cloves of garlic or fresh ginger but I'm
not so keen on those. It's up to you — trial and error is the key.

To make the pickle, wash your veges in your good water, then slice or
chop into small pieces. Put in a clean, non-reactive bowl and sprinkle
with the salt. Rub it into the vegetables and let it all sit for an hour.

Add a sprinkle of the spices, then arrange the whole lot, including
the juices extracted by the salt, into the jar, packing it all in tightly.
I've never made a jar that was too spicy, but I have had jars with not
enough spice, so be generous the first time and see how you go.

Use your good water to fill the jar so it submerges the vegetables but
leaves a 2 cm gap at the top. This gap is very important for the gases to
do their pickling thing.

Close the lid and keep your pickle jar on the bench for a week. By
then the veges should be crisp, sweet and sour, but feel free to leave it
longer if you want a stronger taste. If you haven't got a special pickle
gas-release top, you need to open the lid and burp your jar every day to
let the gas out.

Once you're happy with the flavour, pop your jar in the fridge and visit
often. It will last for 2–3 months.

Shrubs

A shrub drink is an old-fashioned concoction that was designed to slake your thirst. They are traditionally made out of fruit, sugar and vinegar. Dilute the syrup with soda water for a refreshing drink — you can even add a slug or two of gin or vodka!

Cardamom pear shrub

---

4 pears, washed, cored and thinly sliced

2 green cardamom pods

½ cup sugar

¼ cup brown sugar

apple cider vinegar

Put the pears in a glass bowl with the cardamom pods. Add the sugar and stir gently to coat the fruit. Cover the bowl with a clean tea towel and let it sit on your counter for three days, stirring daily. If fruit flies are a problem in your area, cover the bowl and towel with a mesh tent.

Strain the syrup into a measuring cup and combine with the same amount of apple cider vinegar. Pour into a sterilised jar (see page 127) and store for up to 6 months in the fridge.

Strawberry lime shrub

---

2 cups sliced strawberries

1 cup sugar

1 cup apple cider vinegar

zest from 1 lime

Put the strawberries, sugar and lime zest in a sterilised jar (see page 127) and muddle the strawberries with the sugar. Loosely place a lid on the jar and let it sit on your kitchen counter for two days.

Add the apple cider vinegar to the jar and stir to combine. Strain into another sterilised jar using a fine-meshed strainer. Store covered in the fridge for up to 6 weeks.

DON'T FORGET ABOUT the other good bacteria hanging around on your skin to protect you. Hug lots of animals, get dirty, don't wash it all off with high-octane antibacterial washes and, most importantly, snuggle into your grubby children and grandchildren.

As I researched this section I found an article about your mouth microbiome entitled 'The war zone in your mouth!' Part of me thinks this is microbiome hype gone mad, but the article made the point that 'for years we have been trying to kill oral bacteria because we linked it to oral disease, but we now know that up to 90 per cent of bacteria in our mouths is essential for maintaining oral and probably systemic health.' So we're advised to still maintain good oral cleanliness but not to use antibacterial mouthwashes, which kill good bacteria too.

Alternative milks

Finding an alternative to cow's milk is very easy these days and must be a relief for people who cannot tolerate dairy. Today if you order a coffee at a café you can usually get any non-dairy milk you choose: almond, soy, oat, cashew or coconut.

I don't have a dairy allergy and love cow's milk, but in an effort to achieve more diversity in my diet, I decided to swap out some cow's milk and try some others. I was not disappointed — by the taste, at least.

However, reading the labels of some of these milks was a bit of a disappointment. Many of them have only 2 per cent almond or coconut in them. My daughter Pearl was horrified when she heard I was drinking alternative milks and sent me ingredients labels proving that the biggest ingredient in many of these milks is oil.

'Just drink bloody milk, Mum,' she said.

Like mother, like daughter.

Another common culprit in the ingredients label is sugar, which definitely shouldn't be there.

In my efforts to remain processed-food-free, I decided to make my own almond milk, which was surprisingly very easy.

I now have homemade almond milk on my cereal and coconut yoghurt on my Forest muesli in the morning and will often have almond milk in my morning coffee. You do have to heat it before adding it to your coffee or else it will curdle.

Almond milk

This is so easy to make and you get a surprising amount of milk from your almonds. You will need a bag to strain the mixture — an old pillow case is perfect or a smaller cloth bag. You can also try this with other nuts like cashews.

1 cup raw almonds

4 cups water — try to use filtered or mineral water
to avoid additives like chlorine and fluoride

Cover the almonds with water and soak overnight.

In the morning drain and rinse the almonds then put in a blender along with the water.

Blend on high until creamy. There will still be tiny bits of nuts in the mixture.

Strain the milk through a cloth bag to remove the nuts, squeezing the bag to get all the liquid out.

Store in the fridge for up to a week. This makes about 1 litre.

Getting sober

There was a time when I would have read that heading and skipped over this bit. When you are in the habit of drinking, you tell yourself that it's the only fun you get in your busy life. That it is a harmless habit; everyone does it. That people who don't drink are boring.

While I was writing this section, my daughter Hannah asked me what my thirties were like, as she is in her thirties now. I replied that I think I was mostly drunk. I had a baby die, a broken marriage, I met Paul, married, had another baby and pulled together a blended family while editing weekly magazines. Hannah sympathised. Alcohol definitely got me through my thirties so I'm not going to give it a hard time for that.

I recently interviewed TV presenter, broadcaster and musician Anika Moa, who had been sober for 100 days and counting. She told me that stopping drinking was the best decision she ever made.

I know what she was talking about because Paul has been sober for a year and has been saying much the same thing.

There are many reasons people stop drinking, but I think the biggest one is that your mind and body feel better and there is the ability to take back control from something that can start to rule your life.

But it's not easy and it means that for a while you have to steer clear of people who love to drink and really don't like it if you don't.

Social pressure to drink as a group is still very strong in this country and for some reason it's my age group who are doing most of the pressuring. The younger generation seem to have got it sorted and would never pressure each other to drink if they didn't want to.

But I've had people really, really badger me at social functions to drink with them. They won't let it drop, as if the fact that I'm not partaking of the fluid means I've let the side down. On one occasion it was 11 a.m. and I was driving and had just popped in to say hi.

There are some occasions when I give in and say 'Okay, just one', then just quietly deposit it on a table somewhere. Just to keep the peace. It's really annoying actually, not to mention wasteful, so I largely avoid those people now.

I haven't given up completely, unlike Paul. Like many people I love, he cannot have just one glass of wine. One glass leads on and on until there are empty bottles. It's just the way he drinks. He blames his Irish genes.

I am fortunate enough to be able to have one or two and enjoy them and then have a cup of tea. I will also drink more than one if I'm in good company and having a pleasant time. But I have control over what I want to do. Paul doesn't. The wine takes over.

So he stopped, with remarkably little fuss, as is his way. He just stopped one day and that was it. No AA meetings, no relapses. Just stopped. He did the same when he stopped smoking. It would be fair to say that he has transferred his love of evening alcoholic cocktails to a love of evening non-alcoholic cocktails, on which he has become somewhat of an expert, exploring Seedlip and Lyre's non-alcoholic offerings that taste like rum, whisky, gin and so on.

But that's fine. He's happy and has never looked healthier. He's lost weight, doesn't fall asleep watching TV any more and he sleeps well for the first time in his adult life.

And what I found out when he stopped was that I am a social drinker. If you're having a drink I'll join you, but I will not drink alone. It just doesn't make sense. I also don't need to drink every night to be happy. So I go weeks, sometimes months, without a drink when we are together in the Hokianga. And when I catch up with my friends in Auckland I'll have a drink and only once in the past year have I overdone it.

That was me at SPQR in Ponsonby at closing time on a Tuesday, chatting enthusiastically to actress Rena Owen, who was trying to get home after a long day that included a stage performance earlier that night. Sorry, Rena.

When you stop drinking you also have to change the way you socialise. It would be fair to say that Paul and I once operated a fairly social house in Grey Lynn where friends would congregate frequently and the wine would flow and flow and flow. One friend once referred to our home as the Bermuda Triangle because once you entered you couldn't leave sober.

Recently we had a group of friends to stay up north and had plenty of wine and spirits available, but Paul also had some knock-out alcohol-free cocktails for them to try.

When they arrived they all told us that they weren't drinking. These were friends we would drink with regularly just a few years earlier. So we sat at dinner two nights in a row and had lovely conversations and laughs as we always do and noticed very little difference except that we were all in bed by 10.30 instead of 2 a.m.

We've also noticed that hardly any of us drink at family gatherings any more. At our last gathering only two out of the 10 of us were drinking and even then they only drank half a bottle of red wine and took the rest home.

So I think things are changing and I certainly hope so. Alcohol has been a negative in my life. As a child growing up with parents who drank heavily. As a parent trying to keep my drunk children safe. As a partner trying to keep my drunk partner safe. As a friend trying to keep my drunk friends safe. And as a woman trying to keep my drunk self safe.

It's also interesting how many things become normalised when you drink. When a friend went into rehab years ago, I had no idea he was an alcoholic. Then I realised that when I wanted to get in touch with him I rang the 24-hour bar where he could be found most of the time.

Not drinking is freeing on every level. It's just so much better for me not to miss sleep because the alcohol wakes me up at 2 a.m., or not to wake up feeling like shit and regretting saying or doing something I shouldn't have. Lovely.

If you are a drinker that is fine, but do take a moment to think about how you react when a friend isn't drinking. For some it is a terrible addiction and so incredibly hard to give up. For others, like me, it's just that I choose not to. Either way, as a friend your support is not only appreciated but badly needed. Never pressure anyone to drink if they don't want to. They're not boring — you are — especially when you've had too many.

I've just read this back and you're right, non-drinkers can be boring because they get preachy. I apologise for my preaching — please be assured that I don't do this when I'm out. And to non-drinkers who might be tempted to preach, perhaps you could share some gossip or a recipe instead.

A note on addiction

What I have just described is one person giving up the drink and another not drinking much at all. Neither of us were fighting a serious addiction problem. Addiction is something I know a bit about, having supported a few people in and out of recovery, but I can't fully understand it as I haven't been there myself.

What I do know is that addiction is thorough and binding and when it is active it makes people neglect themselves and others they love. It makes them lie. It makes them do things they would never dream of doing sober, to feed that addiction. It is a disease and fighting it takes every bit of strength your soul can offer. And sometimes even that is just not enough.

So my cheerful piece about how we gave up drinking does not apply to those people who really struggle. Who sit in rooms around the country just trying to get through another day. Who head in and out of recovery hoping that this time it will stick. And if you know someone with an addiction, then please be there for them. Don't walk away. Don't tell yourself that they just don't have enough sticking power, that they should try harder. Be there, throughout it all, up and down and in the room with them until they tell you to leave them to it. Which may be never.

A note on Coke No Sugar

I love Coke No Sugar, I'm not going to lie. For a while there when we stopped drinking alcohol we got through an awful lot of it because it's sweet, it's fizzy and it goes down a treat. But while we weren't drinking any calories, we were consuming a lot of artificial sweeteners. The science on that is interesting.

Tim Spector says that the chemicals used to achieve 'zero calorie' drinks 'come from chemicals made from paraffins and all kinds of weird artificial compounds'. The effect of these 'weird' ingredients? They cause our gut microbes to produce certain chemicals that upset our metabolism. 'They essentially counteract any benefit from having zero calories. If you summarise all the trials of putting people on diet drinks as opposed to keeping them on their regular fizzy drinks, there's no difference in weight or diabetes at the end of the year.'

So it is possible — and science has yet to prove this conclusively — that your stomach still thinks the no-sugar drink is a sort of sugar and tries to metabolise it as a sugar of some sort. So you're not drinking zero calories, you're just drinking a chemical cocktail that your gut microbiome doesn't understand.

I still have a Coke No Sugar now and then. I can't help it. Sparkling water with a squeeze of lemon just doesn't do it for me all the time. Read on for some non-alcoholic drink suggestions with fewer chemicals.

Paul's non-alcoholic cocktail recipes

————

As more and more people choose not to drink alcohol, the need for a grown-up substitute beverage has also grown. No one can drink that much fruit juice or soft drink. What's missing from those alternatives is a certain tang that makes a drink something you want to sip rather than quaff.

Supermarkets and liquor stores now have a range of non-alcoholic alternatives that slightly mimic the flavours of gin, bourbon, rum and other standard spirits. Seedlip and Lyre's are the brands you're most likely to find, although supply can be a bit hit-and-miss. They are still not common in country stores, either, so Paul stocks up in town whenever he sees them. A couple of bottles of these along with a pair of shrubs, some bitters and mixers like tonic water will give you a huge variety of drinks you can mix and match to your taste. Here are two to get you started, but do experiment for yourself to find the ones you like best.

Strawberry surprise

————

2 parts Seedlip Citrus

1 part 'Strawberry lime shrub' (see page 152)

3 parts tonic water

generous dash orange bitters

Stir together all ingredients over ice in a chilled glass and serve with an olive or a slice of lemon — or, if you really want to push the boat out, a slice of lemon *and* a slice of orange.

Pear present

_____

2 parts Lyre's White Spirit

1 part 'Cardamom pear
shrub' (see page 150)

3 parts tonic water

dash Angostura bitters

Stir together over ice in a chilled glass and serve with a slice of lemon.

Twinings teabag drinks

_____

*When it's hot, an iced tea is always perfect, but you have to make it with
hot water, then let it cool, then put it in the fridge. Then I discovered
Twinings' cold infusions and bought the whole range, I was so delighted.*

*First, they taste amazing and have lovely flavours like watermelon,
strawberry and mint (my favourite). Second, they have less than 1 g of
sugar per 500 ml. Third, they are made of natural ingredients. And lastly
you just throw them in some cold water with ice, let them sit for a few
minutes, give them a stir and you have the perfect refreshing drink.*

*I was also glad to see that the pyramid teabags, which look like they're
made of plastic mesh, are actually made of a corn-starch-derived material
that will degrade in local authority composting. So while they might not
decompose quickly in your home compost, they will eventually break down
in the rubbish system and not sit around for hundreds of years like plastic.*

Parmesan crisps

Parmesan crisps are so delicious and make a really nice base for chutneys or cheese when you want a snack. I like to top them with some cottage cheese or sour cream then dab with chilli sauce.

Heat the oven to 180°C. Line an oven tray with baking paper.

Using the finest setting, grate the desired amount of Parmesan cheese.

Evenly space tablespoonsful of cheese on the tray, then press them flat with your hand.

If you wish, sprinkle with some flavouring, such as paprika, chilli or celery salt.

Cook for 8 minutes. Watch closely because they burn easily. You want to remove them just as they start going golden.

Transfer to a wire rack to cool. Store in an airtight container for up to a month. They may become a little soft but they'll still taste great.

Building healthy habits

We all have habits that we perform every day. Cleaning your teeth is something you do twice a day because you have always done so. It has become a healthy habit.

When it comes to changing habits, like giving up alcohol or cigarettes, or starting new ones like eating more nuts and seeds, or getting regular exercise, it can take a long time for that habit to kick in and become something we do regularly without even thinking about it.

We used to think that it took three weeks for a new habit to kick in, but recent British research has found that the amount of time it took for a task to become automatic ranged from 18 to 254 days, with a median time of 66 days. That's two months and counting.

The study also found that practising the new thing every day made a big impact on how long it took to become a habit.

It makes sense, then, to start with something easy that you can do every day rather than something you do once a week. Perhaps a daily walk before dinner will become a habit more easily than a full-on gym workout twice a week.

If you're trying to stop a habit, it's also a good idea not to go cold turkey if you can. If you want to reduce sugar in your coffee, have one teaspoon instead of two for a while. Then half a teaspoon instead of one. Or drink one less glass of wine a night for a while. Take it slowly and see if you can harness the power of forming a new habit.

Stack your habits

It can be helpful to attach your new habit to an old one — this is called stacking. If I'm trying to incorporate something new into my life I will do it around cleaning my teeth or having a cup of coffee, which are things I do at the same time each day without fail. I will usually have a swim after my morning coffee if the tide is right and then be back in time for lunch. If I am writing a lot, like working on this book, I will always start writing when I have my morning coffee. There's a lot riding on that cup of coffee.

In the afternoons I try to remember to go over and have a catch-up with my dad, so I attach that to my afternoon cup of tea, which I have at about 3 p.m. I find myself making the tea and then automatically carrying it over to Dad's house now.

Some people practise balancing on one foot while they are cleaning their teeth, then switch to the other foot, or they do push-ups after they've been to the toilet. The possibilities are endless!

Make it easy

We are hardwired to resist things that are difficult. We've all been heading off to the gym and been unable to find our gym gear, or our water bottle, or in my case just my will to live, and so have postponed the trip in favour of a lie down.

If you really want to go for that ocean swim, then the night before get all your gear out and ready. I hang my swimsuit, complete with goggles, watch and swim cap by the door. That way it's ready for me and as soon as I'm in it, like an astronaut going to the moon, nothing is going to stop me swimming.

The same goes for healthy eating. If I don't do the prep and have healthy food available in my kitchen, I will deviate to something quick and easy. I no longer have instant noodles or biscuits in my house for that reason. Actually I do have a packet of biscuits, but they remain unopened until someone arrives for a cup of tea. I think it's rude not to offer something to eat and so they are there just for that purpose, which means I leave them alone. The feeling of embarrassment I would have at not having a plate of biscuits to offer stops me eating them.

I developed my healthy eating habit by having great food around all the time.

Reward yourself

The biggest reward for me drinking less alcohol is waking up with a clear head and no hangover. On the rare occasions when I do succumb I spend the whole next day as a zombie. As well as eating a lot of pies.

So when I go to a social occasion and have just one glass of wine and head home, I take a moment to thank myself for how good I'm going to feel in the morning.

Simply noticing, naming it and feeling it is a good way to reward yourself. That great feeling you get after exercise — notice it and thank yourself for it. If you're eating healthier food, notice how your body is working better and feeling better, and thank yourself for it.

Give yourself a goal. I told myself when I started ocean swimming that if I kept doing it for three months I could buy some really cool goggles that fit the shape of your head so that you never get leaky goggles again. I have those goggles now and every time I put them on it is a reward all over again.

Just do it

But not in the Nike way. The marketing term Just Do It is always accompanied by beautiful, fit people charging off to do something really hard like climb a mountain. My Just Do It means just make a small change one day and see how that feels. It can be substituting your normal muesli for my 'Forest muesli' to get more fibre. See how it feels. Then do something else.

Our lives are not governed by the habits we've had since childhood. Our lives are open to new habits all the time, we just have to do it.

Sleep

There are so many things that can affect your sleep.

Stress and anxiety keep people awake for hours, noise (however miniscule) is not sleep-inducing, light, cats, dogs, children, parties, storms, rain, wind, heat, cold, humidity, dryness, even smells make a difference to whether you get a blissful night's sleep or one that is interrupted and most unsatisfactory. Menopause is the complete anti-sleep bitch in my opinion. Hot flushes will simply not let you sleep.

And the most annoying thing is that we all know that good sleep equals good health.

People who get less than seven hours of sleep a night are more likely to have chronic health problems like obesity, heart disease, diabetes, high blood pressure, stroke, depression and premature death. A recent study even links less than seven hours of sleep with an increased risk of Alzheimer's, which is not news we want to hear.

While we sleep, the brain does back-up work, just like your computer or your phone. It consolidates memories, linking them with old memories and creating paths for you to retrieve memories. It also forms connections between thoughts and ideas.

Another important function of sleep is that it allows the brain to do some mental housekeeping. Sleep cleans out the toxic junk in your brain.

In mouse studies, researchers found that during sleep, the space between brain cells gets bigger, allowing the brain to flush out toxins. While more study is needed, the research suggests that not sleeping can allow toxins to accumulate and may be linked with brain diseases like Parkinson's and Alzheimer's.

Our bodies, meanwhile, relax because our sympathetic nervous system — which controls the fight or flight response — gets a chance to relax.

While you're sleeping, your immune system releases a type of small protein called cytokines. If you're sick or injured, these cytokines help your body fight inflammation, infection and trauma. Without enough sleep, your immune system might not be able to function at its best.

A 2016 survey by Sovereign, an insurance company, found that just over a third of New Zealanders reported not getting enough sleep or that the quality of their sleep was compromised.

The best person to determine how much sleep you need is you. If you feel tired, you probably need more sleep. But science does offer some more-specific guidance. New Zealand's Ministry of Health quotes the US-based National Sleep Foundation's recently updated recommendations based on age: adults up to the age of 65 should aim for seven to nine hours of sleep, while those over 65 need seven to eight hours.

I've read dozens of books on sleep because I'm not good without it. They all promote the same old things. No caffeine after midday, no computers before bed or in bed, have a bath, turn down the lights, do meditation, sniff lavender oil, don't watch TV before bed. The list goes on and on. There are also sleep programmes that might work for you.

What I do know is that breathing is a great help and certainly helps me get nine hours of sleep most nights.

I've come across one more idea that has worked for me, even if it does sound a little bonkers. Check out a TED Talk by a guy called Jim Donovan on YouTube — he says that, for him, the key to falling asleep is rhythm. Being a drummer, he worked out that repetitive tapping combined with deep breathing relaxes the brain enough to fall into good-quality deep sleep.

If you have trouble falling asleep or wake in the middle of the night and can't get back to sleep, I really encourage you to try his 30-second exercise. Over 5.3 million people have watched his TED talk, so I'm thinking there's something there.

Breathe

Last year, I tucked myself up in bed and made preparations to sleep. I turned to Paul to kiss him goodnight and was met with a response I didn't particularly like.

'I don't want to know.'

He said it in a very firm, no-nonsense way, in a voice he uses when I am being totally ridiculous, which to be fair does happen sometimes. This was one of those times because there, trying to give him a kiss, was a woman who had taped her mouth shut with surgical tape — not in a 'full-on duct tape across the whole mouth because I'm being held hostage' way, just a little piece of tape the size of a Hitler moustache placed vertically in the centre of my mouth to keep it closed.

It was an idea I had taken from *Breath: The new science of a lost art* by James Nestor. The book had already helped a friend's anxiety by teaching him how to breathe properly through anxiety attacks. I reasoned that I would use it to help me sleep.

The theory is that by teaching yourself not to breathe through your mouth at night, you will sleep better and stop snoring, and that if you are suffering from sleep apnoea, your symptoms will disappear.

I woke up the next morning feeling amazing. The tape was still in place and I felt that I had really rested. Paul also confirmed that I hadn't snored, so it worked out all right for him in the end.

I interviewed James Nestor, who told me that so much of the science around breathing that has been conducted in the past 50 years has been totally ignored by the medical profession. Many of the breathing techniques that have been studied were also an essential part of medicine for humans 3000 years ago.

'Ancient traditions, from the Indians to the Chinese, believed that if you didn't breathe correctly you would die,' said James, whose pain-

173   Body

staking research uncovered evidence of breathing practices from all over the world. There's tummo breathing, practised in Buddhist traditions, and prana — many of us have come across this at yoga classes — which translates as 'life force' in Sanskrit. The concept of prana was first documented around the same time in India and China some 3000 years ago and became the bedrock of medicine. The Chinese called it 'ch'i', the Japanese called it 'ki', the Greeks called it 'pneuma', Hebrews 'ruah' and Iroquois 'orenda'.

The problem with getting a prescription for breathing exercises during a doctor's visit is that scientists have traditionally been sceptical of these ancient practices.

'It was easy to dismiss because there weren't any randomised controlled trials out there but I did find out that for the past 50 years, researchers at some of our top institutions have been running controlled trials, doing the science, and have proved that this stuff absolutely works,' James told me.

But, like so many things that are good for us, when there is no money to be made from telling people to breathe, the message doesn't tend to make it to the medical establishment.

'I don't really want to point the finger at big pharma but a top pulmonologist at a top university did tell me that the reason we're not being taught this stuff and people don't know about it is that there is no way of making money off it,' said James.

After I talked to James I instituted a regular breathing practice every day and I found it really helped. I now breathe completely differently because it has become a habit. Occasionally if I feel anxious I'll notice that I'm not breathing properly so will take some time to do the breathing practice and get it back to normal. I will also do breathing exercises at night if I find it hard to get to sleep.

These are the two breathing practices I use, but there are many others you can find in James's book or online. I really encourage you to think about the way you breathe as you would think about the way you feed yourself. We tend to think that breathing is just something we do automatically, which is true, but we can help our body breathe better with some practice.

4-7-8 breathing

The following technique, made famous by Dr Andrew Weil, places the body into a state of deep relaxation.

- Take a breath in, then exhale through your mouth with a whoosh sound.

- Close your mouth and inhale quietly through your nose to a mental count of four.

- Hold for a count of seven.

- Exhale completely through your mouth, with a whoosh, to the count of eight.

- Repeat this cycle for at least four breaths.

Weil offers step-by-step instructions on YouTube.

Resonant (coherent) breathing

Resonant breathing is a calming practice that places the heart, lungs and circulation into a state of coherence, where the systems of the body are working at peak efficiency. There is no more essential technique, and none more basic.

- Sit up straight, relax the shoulders and belly, and exhale.

- Inhale softly for 5.5 seconds, expanding the belly as air fills the bottom of the lungs.

- Without pausing, exhale softly for 5.5 seconds, bringing the belly in as the lungs empty. Each breath should feel like a circle.

- Repeat at least 10 times, more if possible.

Several apps offer timers and visual guides for your breathing practice. Many smartphones and watches will give you guiding breathing programmes as well.

Land

'When we try to pick out anything by itself, we find it hitched to everything else in the Universe.'

John Muir, *My First Summer in the Sierra*, 1911

Regeneration

As I'm writing this two people are braving the midwinter weather and planting out a third of our two-acre paddock with 1000 native trees. We've got mānuka, cabbage tree, flax and koromiko going in and six pōhutukawa along the waterfront. I hope I live long enough to one day sit on the beach under their shade with my grandchildren and possibly great-grandchildren.

What I do know is that pōhutukawa live for a thousand years. These trees, along with our extra natives, will help to slow down the rapid erosion we are experiencing on the shores of the Hokianga Harbour. Their roots will filter any run-off before it gets to the harbour and will also set up a network of fungi in the soil that communicate with each other, sending nutrients and warnings of potential danger. Above ground the trees will provide shelter and food for many native insects, lizards, frogs and birds. I hope that in a thousand years someone will also enjoy sitting beneath the shade of my pōhutukawa.

What is happening at my place is known as rewilding or regenerating — I think anyone with a bit of land should have a think about it too. The word 'rewild' was coined in the 1980s by the American conservationist Dave Foreman and it's not without its critics. Rewilders are often dismissed as mad hippies who hanker for a return to nature that is thought impossible. Slowly but surely, many people all over this planet are proving that it's not.

In New Zealand we are a nation of sheep and cows and paddocks. Just a few generations ago, our people were busy clearing bush and gorse to make farmland because that was how this country would survive. Sheep and cows. Dairy and meat exports.

Today we are still dependent on this income. We produce enough food to feed about 40 million people, but only have a population of

5 million — 95 per cent of our dairy, 87 per cent of our beef and 94 per cent of our lamb and mutton is exported. All those paddocks with all that grass are still being put to good use.

My 89-year-old father's generation grew up knowing that a good property is one with British-like, neatly fenced, green flowing paddocks of grass and at home a neatly cut lawn, manicured around the edges.

But now, we're learning that's not such a good idea. We're realising that returning the land to its natural state provides food and shelter for hundreds of birds, insects and fungi. In many cases rewilding attracts birds, animals and insects that were previously on the verge of extinction, and our intensively farmed soil returns to something resembling a living, breathing earth.

When I first had the idea of planting out the paddock, after our time raising cows (more on that later), I rang the regional council to see if there was any funding available.

There wasn't funding for smallholders like us. The council was concentrating on converting huge tracts of farmland, and that was fair enough.

Then I found a local trust, Tiaki Ngā Wai O Hokianga. It was set up a few years ago with the specific aim of growing natives in nurseries, which are then planted on the shores of the Hokianga Harbour to help prevent erosion. After a chat and a donation, we got some plants in and got cracking.

Rewilding is taking place at a huge scale internationally too.

In Sussex, England, conservation pioneers Isabella Tree and Charlie Burrell undertook a rewilding project on the 3500-acre Knepp Estate that Charlie inherited from his grandparents.

For 17 years Charlie did his best to make the estate profitable, but it was impossible to compete with larger, industrialised farms on better soils. Eventually, like many farmers he sold his dairy herd and his machinery to pay off enormous debts and contracted out his land.

In 2002 everything changed for Knepp Estate. It received Countryside Stewardship funding to restore a park in the middle of the estate: 350 acres that had been under the plough since the Second World War. The park restoration provided a chance to look at the land in an entirely different way and suggested the possibility of rolling out nature conservation across the whole place.

It took years for the idea to be wholeheartedly supported by the British government, but Knepp Estate is now a leading light in the conservation movement, an experiment that has produced astonishing wildlife successes in a relatively short space of time and offers solutions for some of Britain's most pressing problems — like soil restoration, flood mitigation, water and air purification, pollinating insects and carbon sequestration.

I read Isabella Tree's book about this project at Knepp, *Wilding*, and was fascinated by the changes that took place. After only a few years, rare birds returned to Knepp, as did rare butterflies and bats. By 2009 there were four bat species, 11 bird species and 60 invertebrate species of conservation importance. Next the couple introduced 53 longhorn cattle, a hardy ancient breed; 23 wild Exmoor ponies, one of Europe's oldest breeds of horse; and 20 Tamworth pigs and 42 fallow red deer. These are all animals that would have roamed wild on that land centuries ago.

A few years later egrets, migrating white storks and black storks, one of the rarest birds in western Europe, visited Knepp. Then came the long-eared and short-eared owls, two breeding pairs of lesser spotted woodpeckers and some peregrine falcons. Red-backed shrikes, which had declined to virtual extinction in the late 1980s, turned up. Next came the small predators like stoats, weasels and polecats, the harvest mouse and many other creatures that had not been seen at Knepp for many, many years.

Isabella and Charlie also planted oak, ash and birch as well as thickets of dog rose, bramble, hawthorn and sallow (a type of willow), which provided the new animals with a smorgasbord of browsing food.

Isabella writes of the changes that came with this new life.

'The feeling was totally different . . . there is density and complexity fizzing with life. Birds and insects throw up a wall of sound. Broken branches, dung, hoof-prints, scratching posts and wallows (pools of muddy water that animals literally wallow in) indicate the presence of large animals that have melted into the bush.'

The nicest part of the book for me was the return of the nightingales. From having no nightingales at all, Knepp became host to between 0.5 and 0.9 per cent of the entire British population. Imagine listening to that!

Next they began restoring original watercourses to the land, breaking down Victorian drainage systems previously thought to manage water in a better way. They smashed all of them and restored 18 ponds and lakes. Diggers were used to remove the canals and naturalise the land. Now at Knepp the water has been allowed to return to its original haphazard and curvy drainage pattern, which has reduced the incidence of flooding.

The UK is also attempting to bring back beavers, which were hunted to the brink of extinction in the sixteenth century for their fur, meat and castoreum, the secretion from scent sacs close to the tail used for making perfume and medicine.

Beavers are described as 'ecosystem engineers' who can ease flooding and increase biodiversity. They are a gift to rewilding and flooding. When introduced, beavers will dig canal systems, dam water courses, and coppice trees and shrubs (which means cutting them back to create space for other species).

Beavers' work reduces downstream flooding because the channels, dams and wetland habitats they create hold back water and release it more slowly after heavy rain. They also keep the water clean and free of pollution by gathering and storing sediment in their dams.

Knepp received permission in 2020 to introduce two beavers from Scotland to the estate.

At the time of writing, beavers were even being introduced into London at Tottenham to breathe life back into deserted marshlands there. Two beavers released at the National Trust's Holnicote Estate in Somerset turned their 2.7-hectare enclosure into a more open wetland by creating diverse habitats that benefit a range of wildlife, including sparrow hawks, grey wagtails, herons, moorhens and kingfishers. They also rather delightfully gave birth to a kit. It's easy to see how just two little beavers can create so much good, and hopefully in the future the UK will be home to many more happy eco-friendly beavers.

Over in Paris they are busy opening up the River Bièvre, which meanders for 35 km through the city underground. It was covered up in the early 1900s but now the local Green Party is working to bring the lost river back to life. They say it will combat climate change, by keeping the city cool. It could also be an oasis for birds, greenery and wildlife.

Mother trees

We already have a lot of native trees growing around our house that were planted in shelterbelts when the house was built 20 years ago.

I'm ashamed to admit that we've owned this place for eight years but I've only recently spent time in the little areas of bush getting to know my trees. Just the other day I found three kahikatea growing in full view of my kitchen window. They were previously hidden by other trees, and can grow to 80 metres apparently so I am very much looking forward to

these three trees making a mark. I read about them in Ngāi Tahu leader Mark Solomon's memoir, *Mana Whakatipu*. His Uncle Ku told him a story about the kahikatea tree and how its shoots and roots grow out and then twist and intertwine, linking the forest.

'So, when the wind comes, they support each other,' says Mark. 'It takes a tree quite some time to actually fall, even when it's dead, because the roots keep holding it up.'

Mark's uncle told this story to encourage the Ngāi Tahu council to support each other through good times and bad.

When I realised the trees were kahikatea and how amazing their complicated, spread-out root systems were, I went down and stroked their bark, introduced myself and promised to look after them, so they could look after each other.

When I told my father about this discovery he immediately knew what I was talking about.

'White pine, it used to be used for butter boxes. They don't have resin so the wood is great for food storage.' I am sometimes amazed at my father's vast knowledge.

One of my favourite things to do is to find seedlings at the base of my trees, which I replant in areas that would normally be covered in grass. I do this without telling my father or Paul because they both like lawns, but I figure there are little bits here and there that really don't need to be covered in grass. So in go flax and karo, which have beautiful tiny crimson flowers in the spring that the bees go mad about. I also transplant nīkau palms and baby cabbage trees. The idea is that these little treasure troves will increase the bush land we have here and help insects, animals and fungi thrive.

If you're not ready to get rid of your lawn, then at least lose the obsession to cut it really, really short. If you let your lawn grow — say, to 14 cm — wild weeds such as daisies, primroses, plantains, dandelions, buttercups and clover will soon grow and flower, then seed. They'll feed and attract birds, bees, mice and insects, not to mention restore your soil to something approaching an ecosystem.

I have a very specific method of transplanting that was developed after reading *Finding the Mother Tree: Uncovering the wisdom and intelligence of the forest* by Suzanne Simard. Suzanne is a forest ecologist and professor at the University of British Columbia, and has spent most of her life trying to convince foresters that trees talk to each other. Suzanne has proved that trees share resources like carbon, nitrogen and water via underground networks of mycorrhizal fungi, a give-and-take arrangement that boosts the health of the whole forest. Her findings threaten common logging-industry techniques like aggressive brush removal and clear-cutting — what she and a colleague called the 'fast-food approach to forestry'.

Her book is yet another story of a woman making great strides in science only to be largely dismissed by the predominantly male culture that surrounds her. They also intimidated her and tried to suppress her work. I became so frustrated on her behalf while reading her book as she revealed that science and industry really need to play nice if we are to save the planet.

When *Nature* magazine published her work in 1997 they called this mycorrhizal fungi network the 'wood-wide web'. Despite Suzanne's findings receiving international recognition, the forest service that employed her continued to mass-clear trees in forests.

She writes: 'The forest was like the internet too — the World Wide Web. But instead of computers linked by wires or radio waves, these trees were connected by mycorrhizal fungi. The forest seemed like a system of centres and satellites, where the old trees were the biggest communication hubs and the smaller ones the less-busy nodes, with messages transmitted back and forth through the fungal links.'

Suzanne proved that in any grove of trees there is a mother tree, which supports the seedlings growing at its drip line. She proved that the mother tree will give preferential treatment to her own progeny but will also help others.

'Maybe society should keep old Mother Trees around — instead of cutting most of them down — so they can naturally shed their seed and nurture their own seedlings,' she says.

'Maybe clear-cutting the old, even if they're not well, wasn't such a good idea. The dying still have much to give . . . old trees store far more carbon than young ones. They protected the prodigious amounts hidden in the soil, and they were the sources of fresh water and clean air. Those old souls have been through great changes, and this affected their genes. Through the changes, they'd gathered crucial wisdom, and they offered this up to their offspring.'

In 2015 Suzanne began the Mother Tree Project, in which she continues her research investigating forest renewal practices that will protect biodiversity, carbon storage and forest regeneration as our climate changes.

After reading her book I took her advice and went outside. I clambered around under my trees and tried to identify mother trees. I couldn't find any mycorrhizal fungi networks because I hadn't read the bit about them being microscopic. But while I was doing this I started noticing other things.

I noticed that fungi of all sorts were growing all around my land. Some were a grey/blue colour and grew in little communities all together. Others were bold and red and toadstool-like. This is good, I told myself.

Then I picked up the soil and smelled it. It was delightful. It was the same smell I get when I wind down my windows during my drive through the ancient Waipoua Forest on my way home. Peaty, sweet and slightly herbal. A good smell.

I dug into a bit of ground with my trowel and found earthworms, another good sign of an active living soil.

I had done nothing to make this happen except leave my trees to grow undisturbed. They had established a network that was keeping them all alive — even though some trees had died and fallen over in the eight years we had owned the property, they were decaying and feeding the bush floor too. Everything has its purpose.

Back to my transplanting method.

Picture for a moment those bags of soil you get at the garden centre. I'm prepared to believe that the compost was alive before it was bagged up but I very much doubt the potting soil was. To me they are sterile, not living. They are simply something to put your plants in and hold them upright. They will not nourish or nurture plants in the natural way they deserve. Some will have little balls of chemical fertiliser in them.

Instead I take my soil from my property, under the trees, as I know there are fungi, worms and good bacteria in it. I plant everything in that.

I used this method when I planted my bulbs out in pots this year, burying them in topsoil harvested from under my trees.

I popped a couple of the dark blue ceramic pots out on my sundeck where I sit most days to have coffee and listen to the birds. One day I was alarmed to see that the soil in the pots had grown a white thread-like fungus over the top. The fungus had also penetrated through all the tiny gaps in the ceramic, so my brand new pots looked as though they had tiny little cracks all over the surface. The fungus had moved in.

In the old days I would have panicked and accused the fungus of planning to rot my tulip bulbs. But instead I welcomed it and waited. This network was going to help my tulips thrive. And it did. All my tulips this year were astoundingly healthy and beautiful.

I know that many people don't have native bush growing on their property from which to harvest living soil, but there are things you can

do if you live in a small property or even in an apartment.

Simply find some native bush — most parks in New Zealand have some natives planted somewhere — and take a handful or two of soil, maybe even a bucket, as long as you're not harming the trees. Add it to your store-bought or homemade potting mix, keep it watered and watch it change shape and feed your plants.

Think of it as making yoghurt or growing a sourdough starter. You are inoculating your soil with valuable fungi, bacteria and maybe a few worms.

The other thing I do is put similar plants together. If I have some lettuce seedlings that have been raised together, I plant them together so that they can keep on talking to and supporting each other. If I'm lifting a native seedling to replant, I take two or three and plant them together. I also take some of the soil they were living in to plant with them to help them adjust. I see that soil with all its fungi, bacteria and worms as the plant's home soil, and so it will feel it is safe and well cared for.

I'm not crazy — I swear it works. All my native seedlings have thrived in their new homes.

Fungi

You may notice that I talk about fungi a lot — there's a reason for that. We tend to think of our soil as an inert medium in which things grow. But it's not. Soil is full of many different organisms, including fungi, which not only provide plants with extra nutrition and support but, as you've read, also form a network beneath the soil that plants use to communicate.

Suzanne Simard proved that trees talk to each other through fungi in the soil, but English biologist Merlin Sheldrake wrote the definitive book on the fungi that live around us, called *Entangled Life: How fungi make our worlds, change our minds and shape our futures*. Merlin is a mycologist who studies underground fungal networks and writes about fungi with joy, which makes his book such an interesting read.

There are more than two million species of fungi in the world and Merlin does an excellent job of describing them, but my interest centred on how to keep them around my place. How could I make sure I was nurturing the fungi in my soil and therefore helping my plants and trees to live their best life?

I was halfway through Merlin's book and having a discussion with Paul about whether either of us would be willing to try magic mushrooms (now known as psilocybin). Michael Pollan, one of my favourite authors, has written two books on this topic — it appears that very soon we will be able to legally have 'trips', as they used to be called in the seventies, in a safe place with a guide at our side.

Then I heard the sound of a quad bike coming down my drive, which usually meant my farmer friend Pauline was popping in to help me with my cows. We went to look at my ailing cow Betty and then had a cup of tea.

When I walked her back to her farm bike with some eggs from my chickens, she reached into the back of her bike and pulled out a blue ice-cream container full of huge field mushrooms.

'I found them up on my back paddock,' she said. 'Here, have them, they're delicious.'

I fried some up for our lunch and we could not believe how amazing these mushrooms tasted. Their mushroomy taste was fresh, light and delightful, and nothing like supermarket mushrooms. I became a fresh field mushroom addict right there and then.

I rang Pauline to thank her and ask if I could help myself to more, which made her laugh. Those in the know realise that mushrooms need particular conditions to thrive, which usually involve lots of light rain and a certain humidity level. They appear overnight so you need to get out early before the cows eat them.

She said that one year there were so many on her paddocks that carloads of people came out from Opononi with buckets to collect them.

I kept a close eye on her paddocks, but to date have not managed another feed of her beautiful fungi. I finished Merlin's book and now work really hard not to disturb the fungal networks I have on my property both above and below ground.

There are main three fungus groups to know about:

Decomposers

I leave dead trees where they fall. They immobilise and retain nutrients in the soil and the organic acids they produce help create organic matter in the soil that is resistant to degradation. I had been deliberately leaving dead trees on the bush floor because the chickens find good insects to eat in them. Recently Paul has been gathering up the wood to chop for firewood, so we've agreed to leave every second dead tree.

Mutualists

Mutualists are the mycorrhizal fungi Suzanne discovered. They form networks through which plants can communicate and share nutrients. To protect these I don't dig or till my garden at all. I simply plant into the soil that is there (which of course means digging a hole) but that's nothing compared with how I used to start every spring by giving my vege patch a thorough digging-over using Dad's gorgeous old rotary hoe from the fifties. This devastates mycorrhizal fungi.

When I first started gardening I followed the old rules that you dig the shit out of your garden before planting. The idea was that you took the topsoil down to the subsoil level to help promote deep rooting, relieve soil compaction and improve the soil by mixing some compost into those deep trenches.

We now realise that this practice came from old English estate gardens with armies of low-paid gardeners. In these modern times when it is just me out there with my spade and a three-metre-square garden it's a ridiculous waste of time, not to mention it kills those wonderful fungi.

Many people are adopting the no-dig garden, not only because it leaves the fungi alone but also because it prevents stirring up weed seeds that then launch into life thanks to your tilling.

I haven't dug my garden over for two years now. Apparently it takes about five years to see the full benefit, so I'm excited to see that happen. Meanwhile I dose the soil constantly with my great compost, mulch with hay and patiently wait for everything to reach a balance.

Pathogens

I don't use any fertilisers as too much nitrogen can hurt fungi; instead I make my own compost and use it sparingly. Fungi thrives on having other microorganisms around, like beneficial bacteria, so I feed the soil with compost and compost tea. And lastly I never ever use a fungicide as this would swiftly kill any fungi in my soil.

I also make piles of wood chips, which decompose over six months — this makes a great mulch and also provides a great home to fungi. Fortunately my dad bought a wood chipper and can be persuaded to sit and chip branches from time to time. I leave it in piles for six months before using it because otherwise the wood chips can be too full of nitrogen. Then I spread it everywhere I can. I never have enough.

Pathogen fungi are not so welcome at my place because they decompose living tissue and kill plants. However, encouraging high biodiversity in my soil and having lots and lots of good fungi around prevents pathogen fungi from taking over and upsetting the balance.

Insects

As children we were taught, for some reason, to fear insects. I'm not keen on stick insects because my brother once put one down the back of my top, for instance. But I quite like spiders and they live all over the beams of our house, killing flies for me. My daughter Hannah used to spend school holidays with her grandmother in Tauranga and came back scared shitless of spiders, a fear she learned from her grandmother.

I wonder if that's why we have stood by and allowed insects to decline by 75 per cent in the past 50 years, according to English biologist Dave Goulson. Dave is about the same age as me and remembers, like I do, a childhood where butterflies, caterpillars and bees were in abundance.

In his book *Silent Earth: Averting the insect apocalypse*, he makes the point that we need 'insects to pollinate our crops, recycle dung, leaves and corpses, keep the soil healthy, control pests, and much more. Larger animals, such as birds, fish and frogs, rely on insects for food . . . Wildflowers rely on them for pollination. As insects become more scarce, our world will slowly grind to a halt, for it cannot function without them.'

We all know that we need to stop using pesticides to try to slow down this decimation of insects around us. Many gardeners like myself are doing this and noticing a difference. As Dave says: 'This is very different from a lot of these big environmental issues where people feel completely helpless. With climate change, if you walk rather than drive, you don't notice the planet getting any better. But plant some flowers in your garden and you actually can see butterflies turning up. It may be tiny, but you've done something positive, and it's worked. If we want to save the planet, start with what's right under our noses.'

We can help the insect world by doing some very basic things. For a start, don't teach your children that insects are scary. Get down in the garden or the earth with a magnifying glass and watch the insects — you'll be fascinated with what they do. Grow swan plants so the monarch butterfly will come and lay its eggs on it — it's always magical to see caterpillars grow and turn into a chrysalis and then become a butterfly.

Insects are all around us. Most of them have very important jobs to do, whether it's catching flies, in the case of my army of spiders, or aerating and enriching the soil, in the case of ants. Ants also recycle decaying insects and animals, and sometimes eat pests that are harmful to your garden. Instead of getting out the poison and killing an entire nest of ants every time they find their way into your sugar bowl, perhaps it would be better to just remove the sugar bowl and anything else you've left out that draws them inside. Flies also do great work outside as scavengers of poo and rotting carcasses, as well as providing food for birds, frogs and lizards.

There is some research that shows that farming flies for animal feed is something to think about in the future. Apparently my chickens would thrive on a diet of flies.

So instead of spraying poisonous pesticides around your home, fit screens over the doors and windows so that the bugs stay outside. We have a metal fly curtain on our main front door that reduces fly populations inside by about 80 per cent.

We also need to regenerate green spaces by planting wildflowers, grasses and trees that help insects thrive. Planting out space that is otherwise just used as a lawn or an abandoned lot does make a difference.

We also need to get over our revulsion at eating insects. Dave points out that about 80 per cent of the world's population already consumes them, and while we happily eat prawns, which have an external skeleton that we remove to get to the flesh, we're not so happy about doing the same with a massive cricket.

Our ancient ancestors certainly ate insects and there is a strong argument for farming more insects for food instead of pigs, cows or chickens. Farming insects is more energy efficient and requires less space and water and they are a healthy source of protein, high in essential amino acids and low in saturated fats. We are also less likely to catch a disease from eating insects.

I once ate ants for dessert when we were dining at the world-renowned Danish restaurant Noma in Copenhagen. Its owner René Redzepi specialises in using locally foraged food in his restaurant and is largely responsible for worldwide gourmet trends like eating seaweed, weeds and berries that we never considered as food.

Lately René's focus has been on cooking up insects like locusts, moth larvae and the ants I mentioned delicately sprinkled on a piece of raspberry shortcake. They were delicious and added a spicy flavour I had never tasted before.

Noma's latest summer menu features bee larvae and plankton (which I'm going to call insects of the sea but I'm probably wrong). What is important is that René has a big influence on cuisine around the world and if anyone can make eating insects take off, he can.

It may be the future of feeding everyone in our ever-growing population.

Worms

A lot of people have worm farms in the city and swear by them. Kiwi Nicole Masters spent years perfecting the worm farm and is helping regenerate thousands of acres of US soil, one ranch at a time.

She is also a guerrilla worm farmer, setting up worm farms wherever she goes. She once owned a worm-farm business so there isn't anything she doesn't know about worm farms, including the fact that worm farms should not leak.

'The perfect worm farm makes no liquid. Any liquid is a combination of the undecomposed food waste dribbling through worm castings. It can contain diseases and nitrates. It also means that you are losing valuable carbon.'

Her advice for constructing the perfect worm farm is simply to cut a large drum in half lengthwise, put a hole in the bottom and keep it just off the ground.

'I feed my worms a blend of pig and horse manure, avocado pulp, cardboard and white wood chips dusted with fine lime and the occasional light additions of rock phosphate and seaweed. If you want to make a liquid, take half a cup of the vermicast, pop it in a two-litre bottle, fill it with water and give it a good shake. Put that on your garden and the plants will love it.'

The agrologist travels around the United States in an eight-metre-long horse trailer with Flynn, her horse, and Rain, her dog, working with ranchers to regenerate their soil.

Regenerative agriculture means that a farmer moves away from intensive farming using fertilisers such as nitrogen and phosphate, herbicides and pesticides and views the farm as a complete entity — soil, water, plants and animals are all part of an ecosystem that needs the right conditions to thrive.

For Nicole, it means 'integrity, restoring natural cycles and transparency of food production systems'.

'Soil doesn't offer the same kind of sexy powerful feeling that blasting a big rocket into space does — well, for most people anyway,' says Nicole.

'There is a whole world under our feet, begging to be explored. It's a world that has been largely ignored and kept out of sight, until more recently. We're spending trillions figuring out how to get to Mars, or

discovering life on other planets, when we are barely comprehending the life we have on earth,' she says in her book *For the Love of Soil: Strategies to regenerate our food production systems.*

One ranch Nicole loves is Alderspring Ranch, which covers 46,000 acres. In the past six years it has doubled its soil carbon levels in a very harsh environment.

'They are doing meat testing and they're finding that their meat, which is produced organically using regenerative principles, is off the scale in anti-inflammatory compounds.'

She says that if ranches like Alderspring with incredibly low rainfall can do it, anyone can.

'Look at the drought New Zealand had in 2019. New Zealand farmers have no resilience, no preparation. They're in drought in two weeks.

'I've done soil samples all over New Zealand and found the water cycles are massively broken down. A recent State of our Environment Report found that 78 per cent of dairy farms in New Zealand were significantly compacted, which is why water doesn't soak in and stay there, which is why we get into drought. But New Zealand has a good rain-fed ecosystem — New Zealand farmers need to start thinking long term.'

Nicole is right to honour the humble earthworm because where there are worms the soil is aerated. Their burrows also create pathways for the movement and storage of water and help plants to establish root systems.

And that's not all. Most recently earthworm scientists have discovered that as worms travel through the soil, they excrete a fluid that helps them to move and digest, hydrate and detoxify. This fluid lines the wall of their burrows and encourages the growth of bacteria and fungi. They also carry good bacteria in their gut. Some studies have shown that worms in sewage treatment plants eradicate harmful bacteria such as *E. coli* and *Salmonella*, converting raw sewage into nutrient-rich organic matter.

Then there is the vermicast that Nicole mentioned. Sometimes called vermicompost, it is a kind of super-fertiliser created from worm castings. Diluting worm castings in water then pouring the liquid on the garden can restore a lot of microbial life to depleted soils. More studies show that the vermicast may also rid soil of toxic pollutants.

Since making compost, I have never seen so many worms on my property. Every time I get a handful of my new, improved compost (see below), a bevy of worms comes with it. As I spread it around my trees and plants the worms go too and hopefully multiply.

When we bought this property it came with a four-metre-long raised garden. Sadly the soil inside it was completely dead, which is a common problem with raised gardens. After a while the soil becomes disassociated with the earth it is sitting on and there is nothing alive in it. Previously this raised garden had obviously been filled with bags and bags of commercial potting mix and it was basically a mix of pumice and sand by the time I got there. As an immediate quick fix I poured more potting mix on it, but within months it was back to being dead. My salad plants did okay but could have done much better.

This was before I had learned to make great compost. My first effort involved installing a compost tower and some worms. I found a bit of downpipe, drilled some holes around the bottom, then immersed it into the soil with about 20 centimetres sticking above ground. I then put some worms in the pipe and fed them bits of food waste every so often. There was an immediate improvement in the soil but just in that area.

Then I realised that in the summer the raised garden had to put up with glaring hot sun every afternoon, which dried everything out and needed far too much watering. So I planted a row of flax in front of it to help shade it. That helped too.

Finally I realised that if I was going to grow nutrient-dense salad I had to keep this soil alive and that meant creating a living, breathing thing, which is hard to do when all the soil is above ground and not connected to the earth.

Every spring I now replace all the soil, which is a lot, with a mix of soil I have dug from around the property, rotted-down wood chips full of fungi and some of my amazing compost, then I water the whole lot in. I also don't make it too deep: instead of filling the whole garden to the top — about one metre — I fill it half-way. I reason this makes it easier for the fungi, bacteria and worms to communicate with the soil at ground level. The sides of the garden also provide shade on hot afternoons. I've noticed that my veges are now much healthier and robust, and less likely to get attacked by insects in the late summer.

I have also planted a bay tree, to act as a mother tree to the garden.

I am hoping that one day, come spring, I will go to do my annual soil replacement and find that I don't need to. I will just need to sprinkle over some fresh compost and it will all survive through the summer. We'll see.

Compost

I deliberately didn't start this chapter with my new religion — making excellent compost — because it's a bit of a niche interest to be honest. It's like stamp collecting: unless you find someone else who is interested in collecting stamps, your conversation is going to fall on deaf ears.

I do hope that you invest a bit of time reading this, because once you get your head around compost, it stays with you for life. You'll grow plants that will resist disease and pests and will provide you with many more nutrients than you get from store-bought vegetables and fruits.

Plus, the simple art of making good compost infuses your life with patience and care. Which are nice things to learn.

Like many people, I have always had a compost bin at the bottom of my garden. But mostly they were big, black plastic bins and mostly they just produced slimy gunk because all our kitchen waste went in there and not much else. Kitchen waste is great, but good compost it does not make. If you are keeping a compost bin simply to recycle kitchen waste, then my advice is to do what they did in the old days and just dig a hole and bury it. Store it in a big bucket with a lid and when it's full take it out the back and bury it. It's quick and easy and doesn't attract flies. It will also improve the soil it has been buried in, so putting it near trees or your garden is a good idea.

But if you are genuinely interested in making compost that will provide your plants and soil with good nourishment, then let's go.

My love affair with compost started when I interviewed Kiwi Bridget Elworthy about her business selling cut flowers in the UK, The Land Gardeners.

Bridget lives in Wardington Manor in Oxfordshire, a manor house she bought with her husband, Forbes, 11 years ago. This is where Bridget began her cut-flower business, growing flowers and driving them to a London florist each week in the back of the car.

Bridget's passion is creating really good compost. She was the first person I had ever talked to who was concerned about making sure the plants we grow are the most nutritious we can make them.

She told me that back in New Zealand, when she and her husband were involved with a family farm, the two things that came up in business meetings all the time were the cost of fertiliser and animal health. She thought that if the fertiliser was working then the animals should be healthy, but they weren't.

Bridget realised that if the soil isn't right, then you're not getting

nutrients up to your plants. Even though it might look green and taste good, without a nutrient-dense soil it's not that good for you.

This led Bridget to our very own Kay Baxter from the Wairoa-based Koanga Institute, who Bridget described to me as the 'superstar of compost'.

She encouraged me to do Kay's two-hour online compost course and it changed my life.

As I sat watching Kay on my laptop I had no idea that my life as a gardener was about to change for the better.

Kay has huge gardens that are run by teams of people, and so her method of composting is achievable when you have acres of ingredients to call upon. She makes enormous compost cakes in the middle of a field. Carbon-rich corn stalks are layered with bone dust, which is made by collecting bones in a bucket then burning them for hours and crushing them. Mountains of topsoil and other ingredients are then added in a very specific amount and manner. The cake ends up standing about two metres high. Kay waters it, then sticks a thermometer in it with the aim of it reaching 50°C — hot compost breaks down really fast. In a few months she has compost that has exactly the right amount of carbon and nitrogen, as well as everything else the soil needs to be healthy.

She works all this out with meticulous calculations on a whiteboard, so that every bit of compost she makes does the best job it can.

Once I had finished the course I knew there was no way in hell I was going to be able to do that on my small property. I did plant some carbon-rich corn just to go in my compost, but I adjusted Kay's formula to fit my own situation.

One of her big things is giving the compost air to breathe, which is why her compost cakes stand out in the open with just a few poles around the perimeter holding it all in. Cramming your compost ingredients inside a black plastic compost bin is not going to work —

you're not going to get good bacteria, fungi and insects thriving in a hot, claustrophobic, humid mess.

Fortunately I have three large compost bins made out of wooden slats, as they did in the old days, which give my compost plenty of room to breathe.

I cleared one of them out and made it my test compost bin. In went some good-quality topsoil I'd found, which had worms and fungi clearly growing well in it. Then in went layers of chicken manure from under the tree where the chooks all sleep. Then a layer of seaweed. Then a layer of lawn clippings. Then a layer of cow poo from the paddock, then a layer of spent tomato plants and other unwanted plants from the vege patch and a lot of comfrey, which grows all over my place. Then every week I added a layer of whatever I could lay my hands on. When the corn had grown I threw that on. If there had been rough weather I gathered a wheelbarrow full of seaweed and threw that on. Every week I found something to put on there and tried to keep it layered so that it could breathe. Sticks and rotted wood chips created a porous layer that allowed the air through. And I always tried to make sure a manure layer was followed by a green layer like lawn clippings, garden waste or seaweed.

I bought a compost thermometer and stuck it in, fully expecting to reach Kay's 50°C, but it never did. The compost's temperature hovered around 30°C.

Some people recommend turning compost to help it along but I don't agree. I think the less the compost is disturbed, the better the fungi, worms, insects and bacteria grow. You do have to be very careful to make sure you give it plenty of layers of sticks, however, to allow it to breathe.

I had no idea if this would work, but within months I could see that something good was happening. For a start, the pile began to rapidly reduce in size. In a few weeks it had sunk by half. Then, when I tentatively stuck my spade in at the bottom and pulled out some compost, it was dark, friable and full of worms and lots of other weird bugs. Most importantly it smelled really earthy, like good compost should. It was working!

I now use this haphazard method for the other two bins as well, and I'm getting really good-quality compost year round. I can see the effect it's having not only in my vegetable garden but also across my land. I dump it everywhere. Under trees, in the orchard, on the roses, in the flower garden.

On top of that I also have my compost tea, which I make in two big rubbish bins. I fill the bins with comfrey, seaweed and cow poo and leave them to simmer away, creating magic and a disgusting odour. They each have a bug in them now, similar to the mother I have in my cider vinegar bucket, and I know that as long as I keep that fed it will continue to deliver wonderful microbes and nutrition for my soil. It goes a long way when diluted with water to the colour of weak tea. I always use this as a soak for new plants before they go in the garden and as a welcome watering-in tonic.

As Bridget pointed out, growing food with good nutrient levels is well worth the effort. The lettuce you buy at the supermarket might look great, but it won't compare in both taste and nutrition to the one you have just harvested out of healthy soil.

If you are using a plastic compost bin my advice is to throw it out and plead with someone to build you an old-fashioned wooden one with slats you can slide up and out when needed. I've seen really good ones built simply out of packing crates, so that's another idea for you to explore. If you have room, then watch Kay's course and go for the compost cakes. They look like fun!

If you don't live, like I do, with chickens and cows who generate plenty of manure, then be adventurous and see if you can find someone who does and who won't mind sharing a bit of their supply with you now and then.

If you live in an apartment or only have a tiny garden, then bokashi is a great system for small-quantity recycling of scraps. Bokashi involves throwing your kitchen waste in a bucket then sprinkling it with sawdust that has been impregnated with beneficial microbes, which flourish in anaerobic, acidic environments but don't smell.

Eventually you will have a bucket of what is called pre-compost, which you can then bury in your garden (or someone else's garden if you are in an apartment). It breaks down beautifully, feeding that little area of soil.

Moon gardening

We all know that gardening by the moon is a good thing, and it makes sense. It's not hard to understand that the moon at its various stages pushes and pulls water due to the changing force of gravity. That is why when there is a full moon we have a high tide, and when there is a new moon the tides are lower. It isn't woo-woo stuff, it's science.

But moon gardening is something I hadn't really plugged into because I hate doing anything prescriptive. Following a timetable or organising my month around certain gardening activities just makes me stressed. So when someone would say to me 'Oh it's a new moon, time to dig and cultivate,' I'd mainly ignore them.

But slowly and surely, as I was swimming most days and noticing the tides, I started to think about the power of the moon as something quite practical rather than something airy fairy.

So I read *The Natural Gardener: A lifetime of gardening by the phases of*

the moon by John Harris, which explained it all to me.

To be honest, the start of the book is a lot like listening to a lecture by my father on the 'old ways' and why they were much better. John has more than a bee in his bonnet about how hard it is to make everyone realise that gardening by the moon is a good thing to do, so we hear a lot about his battles and how he won every one of them! He also recommends digging up your garden, which I don't do because I don't want to decimate my garden's fungal networks.

But eventually, he gets around to explaining how moon gardening has been around for centuries — and he even has quite an impressive chapter on Māori moon gardening traditions, which surprised me coming from an old Brit.

He explains that at its most basic level, gardening by the moon is all about the water table. So don't think moon gardening will affect your plants in pots, because it won't. They have to be in the soil and have access to the water table.

Gravity is at its weakest with a new moon so the water table at that time is low — so it's not a good idea to plant root crops as there won't be much water available to them.

Slowly, as more of the moon emerges, the water table rises. After it peaks at the full moon, it decreases again.

There are so many instructions to do with each phase of the moon that it is hard to follow it all without a moon calendar. I found a very lovely one from countrytrading.co, which looks like it came straight out of the American *Whole Earth Catalog* magazine in the seventies. It has two rotating circles so that you can set the date against what stage the moon is at.

On the following page I have detailed what it says.

New moon — when there is no moon in the sky, which means rising vitality in the garden

- dig and cultivate
- prepare for a very fertile time
- delay sowing other than grass
- do all odd jobs.

First quarter — when the moon moves to a half moon, when gardening is most prolific

- no root crops
- plant peas, beans, cauliflowers, cauliflowers, cabbage, tomatoes, pumpkin
- don't prune — causes dieback
- take cuttings.

Full moon — when you see the full moon in the sky, which means germination will be weak

- cultivate only
- good for all root crops
- grass can be sown
- spray now.

Last quarter — when the moon moves back to half, which means a barren period

- low vitality, avoid planting and sowing (will go to seed)
- weed
- prune
- put in all root crops, especially swedes, carrots, flowers and grass seed
- spray now.

As you can see, the month is divided into four weeks with specific planting instructions for each week. That's nice if you have a lot of time on your hands, which I don't . . . yet.

The moon calendar might tell me to prune my roses in the last quarter, but that might be the week I have to be in Auckland for work so they get pruned when I get back.

I really want to follow this calendar properly, but for now I have it on my wall in the kitchen and I glance at it each day and make a mental note about what to do, then forget and then go out in the garden and plant some carrots in totally the wrong quarter!

When done properly I agree this can bring better results in the garden, and it's something to work on. Meanwhile I look at the moon every night and note where it is in its cycle and that feels nice. I like that I'm properly noticing the moon every day, and I look forward to one day glancing at the moon and automatically knowing that I need to plant the spuds.

Weeds

Along with composting, I have developed a new attitude to weeds. Traditionally, weeds are the gardener's enemy, robbing nutrients from your plants and smothering them. But weeds are plants too, and many of them are there for a very good reason. They are also the main reason why home gardeners bring glyphosate on to their properties in the form of Roundup. We now know that Roundup (or any weedkiller using glyphosate) is to be avoided at all costs, for both your health and the soil's.

When you step back and look at weeds, many of them can be eaten in salads, used as medicine and left alone to heal your soil.

Australian weed researcher Kate Wall has worked out how to manage weeds, and has written a book about it called *Working with Weeds: A practical guide to understanding, managing and using weeds.*

She says: 'I have come to appreciate weeds as delicious, fresh food, as medicine, as critical habitat, as a guide to how to fix my soil, or just for their beauty. Sure, there are weeds I still would prefer not to have in my garden, but these are a valuable source of compost, if nothing else. Many plants that I once built a career on eliminating, I am now gleefully encouraging in my own garden. My career is so much more joyous and expansive now that it is focused on celebrating life rather than eradicating it.'

Kate says that traditionally weeds were considered as garden 'robbers', taking valuable water and nutrients away from other plants.

'If we instead consider that plants grow better in a community that helps each other, the idea of weeds as robbers holds less water. In fact, many weeds are important soil improvers. They are able to colonise and exploit soil conditions that other plants cannot. They can do this as a cover crop of weeds alone, or they can be useful soil improvers interspersed with the crops or flowers. As many of the weeds are deep-rooted, their roots are not operating in the same soil space as the garden plants (or crops) and therefore there is no competition for resources.'

As we now know, thanks to the work of Suzanne Simard, plants can share nutrients through root-exchange mechanisms that rely on interactions with soil fungi.

Kate says that many weeds have the ability to extract minerals from poor soil. They are able to make these minerals more available to the plants around them via this fungal network, which is a real bonus for those nearby plants.

I love this story from Kate, who works as a gardener: 'I have recently been working on restoring an old, weedy garden. Roses were smothered by weeds. In uncovering the roses, I found one had a false mallow growing at the base of the rose. This weed has been allowed to stay. It is a low-growing plant that shades the soil around the rose, acting as living mulch. It flowers well and helps bring in beneficial insects to the rose. It also has very deep roots, which help forge a way down for the rose roots, in doing so maintaining a living soil biota deeper into the soil. This particular rose plant was not just the healthiest of all the roses in this patch, it was at least five times the size of the others and is never without a flower. Even if you can't agree that the weed growing at its base is helping the rose, it is clear that it is not doing any harm at all.'

Fired up by Kate's book, I decided to let all the weeds grow in my orchard over the summer. I watched as dock took up residence as well as the standard kikuyu we get in the north. I did some research on dock plants and found that they have a large tap root — which we now know is good for breaking up soil. You can also eat the leaves, which taste a bit like spinach and are very nutritious, containing more vitamin C than oranges and more vitamin A than carrots. They also contain vitamins B1 and B2, and iron.

I didn't eat them, but it was nice to know I could.

In the end my orchard became so overrun with weeds that it really looked quite hideous. I had a friend over and showed them my weed experiment and they simply asked 'Why?'

It was a reasonable question.

I did leave my vegetable garden full of weeds over winter though. Normally you are encouraged to 'tidy up' the garden in autumn and leave it fallow during the cold months with bare soil. But I decided to let anything grow as it was going to be better for the soil than nothing at all.

When spring came, the weeding wasn't pleasant but it all went on the compost. One tip I learned from Kate is if you have a weed with a long tap root that makes it hard to pull out, keep a sharp knife with you and simply cut the weed off about 1 cm below the soil. The tap root will break down and keep your soil nice and friable, passing on any good nutrients while it's at it.

Another advantage of growing weeds in the summertime is that many are grasses and go to seed, which birds, especially my chickens, love to eat. So the weeds are providing valuable food too.

I think we are still a while away from gardeners welcoming weeds into their precious plots, but I can see a day when we are at least a bit more accepting and understand that it's really not necessary to kill them with a chemical toxin.

Another thing you can do in your garden to discourage weeds is to grow dense, tough, low-growing plants that will take over the space and smother any attempts to grow through it. Plants like thyme, Australian violet and leptinella (a low-growing fern-like plant) are great weed preventers.

Slugs and snails

I remain mildly suspicious of proponents of the kind of gardening I'm following — organic, nutrient-dense — who say that plants grown this way don't get bugs and diseases. My plants still get slugs and snails, which even the most nutritious and healthy plant cannot resist. So I still use snail pellets — but sparingly and only where my hens can't find them. I use the ones that are ferric (iron) EDTA-based because they are less harmful to wildlife than the ones that contain metaldehyde.

The problem with this is that I am also killing the types of slugs and snails that aren't going to eat my lettuce. According to Hayley Jones, an entomologist and the slug and snail expert at the Royal Horticultural

Society in the UK, only eight or nine of the more than 40 slug species in the UK are a nuisance; of the 100 or so types of snail, 'probably only three of them are problematic in gardens,' she told *The Guardian*.

'The others either don't do much damage, or they eat other things like algae or fungi.' Some slugs and snails can be beneficial 'because they eat rotting material so they're all part of the recycling process in the garden. They all get tarred with the same brush, but they are much more interesting than that.'

I'm making a very broad assumption that we have most of those species of slugs and snails in New Zealand too. One we definitely do have is the leopard slug. According to Hayley, 'The leopard slug is very territorial, which is where its reputation for being a cannibal comes from. It doesn't actually eat other slugs, but it will attack them for encroaching on its territory.' The leopard slug may therefore actually help to protect your plants by acting as a guard slug.

A good habit to get into, and one children love, is to go out in the evening, particularly if it has rained, and collect all the snails and slugs in a bucket.

Some people then release them into the bush or far away from their gardens or, as I have started doing, put them in the compost bin where they can munch and decompose to their heart's delight.

Saul Walker, the head gardener at Stonelands House in Devon and host of the gardening podcast Talking Heads, collects slugs and snails from plants, under and around pots and from the greenhouse, then moves them — although, as he points out, he does have the benefit of 25 hectares of land. 'I throw them in the woodland. They don't make their way back, I don't think.'

I also feed some to the chickens, which gives them a good protein boost. When I have bugs in my garden, particularly the green stink bug that always turns up on my tomatoes at the end of summer, I open my vege patch to the hens and let them go for it. They will happily seek out all the bugs and eat them first — the trick is to get them out before they turn their gaze on to my ripe tomatoes.

Another idea is to encourage snail and slug eaters like frogs into your garden. We have a big pond that acts as a frog nursery every summer. First we hear the mating call of the green and golden bell frog, which sounds a bit like a motorbike revving. Then we see the tadpoles hatch and eat all the weed. That's when I throw in bits of lettuce, grass clippings or any green I can find around the property to feed them. Eventually the tiny frogs emerge and head off into our gardens. Our cat Dickie catches a few — I know this because he often turns up with a ring of pond water around his neck where he has stretched as far as he can without having to get wet to catch one. Wild birds also feast on them. But I think many of them live on to become eager slug and snail eaters.

The other idea is to grow robust plants to a decent size before you plant them out. If stronger, bigger plants get nibbled, 'they can outgrow it,' says Saul. If he has vulnerable seedlings that have been sown directly, he also sows a line of lettuces nearby to distract slugs and snails. 'We need to try to get over this idea that we're the supreme species on this planet and accept the fact that other creatures have a right to enjoy their time on Earth as well. That's a much more balanced way of looking at it rather than just waging war on everything that moves.'

Growing from seed

The ultimate for any gardener is collecting seed from plants you have grown and then using that seed to grow next year's veges and flowers. The theory behind this is that once a plant has grown in your neck of the woods, it passes genetic information on to its offspring (the seeds)

and so they come pre-programmed to your unique garden. The much missed Graham Brazier from Hello Sailor taught me that — he was quite the horticulturist in his time as well as a great musician and poet.

But sometimes seeds just don't take, or they get too damp and rot, or the light isn't right and it just won't happen for you. Other times you absentmindedly chuck some seeds on a bare patch of garden and come back a week later to find a lush crop of mesclun.

Since I've started making my own seed-raising mix I have had much more success with seeds, and by the time I plant the seedlings into the garden they are strong and ready to go. I try to use my own seeds but also, like most gardeners, send an order off to Kings Seeds every spring and can't resist trying new varieties of plants, particularly tomatoes.

DIY mixes for your garden

---

*It is really easy to make your own seed-raising mix, as long as you
sift it before you plant any seeds. You don't want a big clump of soil
sitting on top of a delicate little seed trying to send up a shoot.*

*This how-to guide is very loose but it does involve using perlite and
vermiculite. You might be thinking that this is a ridiculous thing to include
as you will never find it, but conveniently, bags of perlite and vermiculite
are found in garden centres for people who are into hydroponics. Perlite
looks and feels like Styrofoam but is actually made from volcanic glass.
It is a great addition to seed-raising mix because it adds drainage and
stops your seedlings from rotting. Vermiculite is the dry flakes of a silicate
and it protects young seedlings from fungi yet also holds some water.*

*Mixing perlite and vermiculite with some good compost from
your garden makes a great seed-raising mix that is nutritious
and will help your seedlings grow fast and furiously.*

DIY seed-raising mix

---

2 cups good-quality compost

1 cup perlite and vermiculite blend

Sift your compost so that there are no lumps. You don't need a fine sieve from the kitchen, just something that will make the soil fine rather than lumpy.

Mix with the perlite and vermiculite and plant away.

DIY potting mix

Use the same recipe as for the seed-raising mix, but add about 1 cup of coir (coconut husk). You can buy coir at the garden centre. It helps grow a good root system because it doesn't rot quickly and creates air pockets in the soil.

Perlite, vermiculite and coir are all sustainable and great for the environment.

Urban outdoors

Not everyone has a large property to play with and plant trees and gardens as I do. But all is not lost. You can harness some green space, and the positive health outcomes it brings, even if you are in a city flat or apartment.

A really easy thing to do is plant out window boxes, which you can hang from your window ledge, with either some cacti and succulents or hardy annuals like cornflowers, cosmos and marigolds.

If you have a small balcony or somewhere you can keep pots, then head straight for lavender. It will give you a gorgeous scent on a hot afternoon and it can handle baking sun and drought. I have had a lavender bush in a large terracotta pot for 25 years. It has seen some dim times when I forgot to water it, but it always comes back and with the occasional trim keeps on delivering.

Indoor plants are experiencing a renaissance — Paul and I are somewhat horrified to see the monsteras that used to grow in our homes as children in the sixties returning in abundance. We even have one that our daughter 'gifted' to us when she moved to Wellington. We don't particularly like it but we put it by our front door, in memory of our childhoods, and it's thriving.

I also have a thing for moth orchids, those ones you buy at the garden centre for Mother's Day, or are gifted by friends. Usually they look amazing and graceful and delicate, and then they die. Somehow I've managed to work out how to keep them alive and I can even separate them to grow more — don't water them too much, and keep them somewhere like the bathroom where they get a bit of filtered light and a lot of humidity.

Grow your own medicine cabinet

One of the things I experiment with a lot in my garden is growing stuff that heals us. One year I made a comfrey oil, which works wonders on skin complaints and itchy bites. I also grow proper peppermint for peppermint tea, which is fantastic if you have an upset tummy. Lemon balm grows freely around my place — I use it to make a great stomach and nerve settler.

Here are some healing plants you can grow at home.

Kawakawa

Kawakawa is a native shrub you will find growing in most native bush, and often in parks that have been nicely planted with natives. It likes to grow in dappled shade and has heart-shaped leaves. It has a peppery taste when crushed and eaten. Māori have used this plant for years to heal skin infections and stomach upsets. I use it as a poultice and a tea — the poultice will draw out a skin infection and the tea will help with stomach upsets.

Comfrey

It's not hard to find comfrey growing somewhere, as it thrives like a weed. I have some in my garden that I have to keep in check, but it makes a great addition to my compost tea for the garden. I also make a terrific oil out of it; it's well known for its skin-healing abilities. When I'm gardening I get a lot of scratches and insect bites and this oil has proved to be a winner for making sure they heal quickly and don't get infected. In the old days, comfrey was used in many healing concoctions because it contains allantoin, which is thought to increase the speed at which wounds heal. This is such an easy oil to make.

Kawakawa poultice

———————

Pick a couple of leaves, preferably with insect holes as they will be the strongest. Rip them up, then give them a good bash with a mortar and pestle. When they become mushy and you've released their healing oils, grab a teaspoonful of the mush and apply it to the infected area.

Wrap with a bandage and replace it every 12 hours. The infection should begin to reduce within a few hours.

Kawakawa tea

———————

Collect four or five leaves and rip them up into a small teapot or a cup with a lid (you can just put a saucer on your cup if you like). Pour on boiling water and leave to steep for 10 minutes. Pour or strain into another cup and add a bit of honey to taste.

This tea does wonders for indigestion or nausea. It's also a good anti-inflammatory tonic if you are under the weather.

Comfrey oil

---

1 large glass jar (Agee if you have it)

comfrey leaves

olive oil

On a dry day collect the comfrey leaves and chop up into pieces. Fill the jar with them, pushing them down so that they are quite tightly packed into the jar. Pour over the olive oil until you have reached the top, then use a fork to push the comfrey down again to release any air and make more room for the oil.

Put on the lid and sit the jar on a sunny windowsill. In the summer with hot sun this will be ready in 3 weeks; in winter it will take about 6 weeks.

Strain the leaves from the oil and put the oil in a dark glass bottle. Use on any skin complaints or simply rub all over your skin as a lovely conditioner.

Peppermint

This is very different to the English mint we all grow in our gardens to use in cooking and for mint sauce to have with lamb. Peppermint makes the most delicious peppermint tea and is well worth planting in your garden as it will come back year after year. Peppermint has many medicinal benefits, but I find that a strong cup can be quite soothing for an upset tummy.

Lemon balm

I love having lemon balm in my garden simply so that I can squash a few leaves and inhale its wonderful smell. I use it primarily for colds. Like peppermint, it is also quite calming.

Make a tea as for peppermint tea or try adding it to fruit salads and cordials.

Nasturtium

I recently bought some seeds for rather exotic nasturtiums with purple, cream and dark chocolate flowers. But it's mostly the variety with orange flowers that grows everywhere at my place, especially in winter when I let it take over my vege patch. Nasturtium is great in the garden as it has a strong smell that repels some pests. I mostly use it in salads — its leaves taste like rocket and its flowers look lovely sitting on top. I will often pick some leaves to add to a sandwich as well.

Nasturtium is also a great skin healer, so infusing the leaves in a tea can make a great facial wash if you suffer from acne. It was also used in old times for persistent coughs. Make a strong tea as you would peppermint tea.

Peppermint tea

Gather a large handful of peppermint leaves and put them in a teapot or cup. Pour over boiling water and leave to steep for 5 minutes.

Add a slice of lemon if you like, or some honey to sweeten. You can also add milk to make the tea creamy.

Rosemary

A few years ago I decided to plant a rosemary hedge along one side of my vege garden. The eight plants loved their home and are now over a metre high. I am supposed to trim them down into a neat hedge but instead I've just let them grow as they would naturally. They look a bit unkempt but I love them and often place my bed linen over them to dry in the summer so that the fragrance infuses my sheets.

Rosemary is steeped in culture and history. Ancient Greeks believed that it improved memory, so students would wear it in their hair and as garlands around their neck when taking exams. Shakespeare writes about it when Ophelia says 'There's rosemary, that's for remembrance. Pray you, love, remember.' And at weddings in the past a bridesmaid would plant a sprig from her bouquet to be used by any daughter of the marriage on her wedding day. It's just too lovely.

In the kitchen, rosemary works well with roast meats and potatoes and it flavours oils, marinades and sauces. You can also sprinkle its beautiful blue flowers on salads, fresh fruit and cheeses. Spear a camembert all over with sprigs of rosemary and garlic, then bake until creamy. Delicious.

As a first-aid herb, rosemary is antiseptic so it's ideal to rub on sores and bites, and you can add sprigs to the bath to alleviate aches and pains. It also makes a great hair rinse for brunettes.

Lavender

Lavender has a bit of an old-lady reputation, which it doesn't deserve. A sprig of lavender with its delicate lilac flower rubbed between the palms gives off such a wonderful perfume and really lifts your day.

Like many useful herbs, lavender is native to the Mediterranean but because it is a hardy wee plant it survives all over the world, and tends to quite like conditions in most of New Zealand.

Rosemary hair rinse

Get an old jar (Agee if you have it) and pack it full of rosemary branches. Include the flowers if you want lots of fragrance, but make sure there are branches in there too as the wood seems to add something to the mix. Pour boiling water on top, put the lid on and leave to steep overnight.

Use 1 cup rinsed through your hair after washing and conditioning, to further condition and add shine. It will keep in the fridge for a few weeks.

The Romans used lavender to perfume their baths; it's thought that its name came from the word *lavare*, which means to wash. Ancient druids used lavender flowers in their love potions and burned branches of it during childbirth to cleanse the air, calm the mother and bless the baby.

Lavender makes a great essential oil that can be used to treat headaches, help sleep and reduce anxiety. It is also a great healer for cuts, rashes and insect bites. You can also use it in cooking — it's particularly delicious in shortbread and vinegars.

Bees and butterflies are very fond of lavender flowers so a lavender bush or two in your garden is a great idea.

Plant your lavender where it will get lots of sun and have good drainage. Remember to prune it once a year to maintain a good shape and good growth.

Lavender oil

The essential oil you buy is made by extracting the oils with heat, but this is a very simple oil you can make at home, similar to comfrey oil.

1 large glass jar (Agee if you have it)

10–12 sprigs of lavender flowers (make sure you use an old-fashioned lavender like dentata, which has a strong fragrance)

vegetable oil such as safflower or olive

On a dry day collect the lavender flowers and fill the jar with them, pushing them down so that they are quite tightly packed into the jar. Pour over the olive oil until you have reached the top, then use a fork to push the lavender down again to release any air and make more room for the oil.

Put on the lid and sit the jar on a sunny windowsill. In the summer with hot sun this will be ready in 3 weeks; in winter it will take about 6 weeks.

Strain the flowers from the oil and put the oil in a dark glass bottle.

Sage

Sage is a bit of a rock star in the herb world. It has been loved for centuries not only for its ability to make pork taste amazing but also for its medicinal properties, which range from easing sore throats to promoting longevity. In Ancient Greece and Rome, sage was eaten daily as a way to ensure a long life. Indigenous North Americans burn bundles of sage, known as smudge sticks, to purify an area. You can buy smudge sticks in health shops to purify your home if you have just moved in or you don't like the feel of something there.

These days we know sage has antibacterial, antiseptic and digestive properties, so we grow it to enhance the flavours of our food and also for medicinal purposes.

Grow sage in full sun and well-drained soil. It comes from the slopes of southern Europe, so the more Mediterranean your garden conditions, the happier it will be. Cut it back after flowering, but not until after the bees have had their fun with the flowers. Use sage as a companion plant for carrots and brassicas.

There is an old wives' tale that a strong woman rules a household where a sage bush thrives. However, she must not plant the sage herself or it will bring bad luck.

Use sage in the kitchen with pork, in a risotto, or with venison, duck, poultry and oily fish. Potatoes love sage, as do carrots, beans, eggplant and tomato sauces. You can also use sage flowers in salads or fry sage leaves in butter before sprinkling them over your food.

A sore throat will respond well to some sage tea (see next page). If you have dark hair, you can also pour the cooled tea through your hair after shampooing, to condition and add shine. Leave it in for 10 minutes, then towel-dry your hair.

Sage tea

4–5 sage leaves

250 ml boiling water

Steep sage leaves in boiling water for 5 minutes, then strain and add honey and lemon. You could also add a few mint leaves if you like.

Sip slowly, or let it cool and use it as a gargle.

Coriander

As we throw coriander leaves into our guacamole we are unlikely to pause and congratulate it for being one of the most ancient herbs around. This remarkable herb, which some people claim tastes like soap, has been cultivated for 3000 years and is now popular in most cuisines around the world.

Coriander seeds are a must-have for curries and the spice base garam masala. The roots are popular in Thai cooking and the leaves are divine when added at the last minute to salads and Mexican food.

Over the years we have used coriander for many medicinal purposes as it is antibacterial, anti-inflammatory, a good digestive, expectorant and fungicidal. The orange-scented seeds can be chewed as a breath freshener, and essential oil of coriander is great for muscular aches and pains.

Grow coriander from seed in a light, well-drained soil in sunny and dry conditions. The key to having coriander leaves always at the ready in your kitchen garden is to sow seed at fortnightly intervals, because coriander just loves to bolt to seed in hot weather. Let it bolt, then collect the seeds for next season.

Lemongrass

I planted a couple of lemongrass plants a few years ago and now they take up a large corner of my vege garden. They love it there right next to the lemon tree and are about two metres high.

If you do a lot of Asian cooking you will use lots of lemongrass. It's also a really good mosquito repellent and lemongrass tea will treat digestive problems.

If I get a cold I will make a tea of ginger, lemongrass and lemon juice with a bit of honey. Lemongrass tea is also a soothing delight on its own.

Lemongrass insect repellent

Collect a large bunch of leaves from your lemongrass plant. Put in a saucepan with 500 ml water, put on the lid and boil until the mixture is yellow.

Cool, then strain the mixture into a spray bottle.

Lemongrass tea

Take three lemongrass shoots and smash the bulbous ends to release the oils. Put in a mug and pour boiling water over. You can leave some leaves in there too if you like.

Cover and let steep for 5 minutes.

Chilli

Many of us grow chillies over summer and enjoy using them in our cooking. Next time you have a cough, add a chopped-up chilli to your lemon, honey and ginger drink and it will really help clear out that mucus.

The best use of chilli at my place is as a plant spray to repel caterpillars and ants.

Chilli plant spray

3–4 chillies

1 tbsp dish detergent

1 litre water

Grind chillies with dish detergent. Add to water, infuse for 30 minutes, then strain into a clean sprayer.

Water

It's all very well talking about keeping our land alive, but we are also surrounded by beautiful oceans. All across our land are rivers and estuaries, which are just as important to our environment as the land.

I live by the sea on the Hokianga Harbour, which is pretty clean according to tests taken during the summer. We don't have a lot of people living here but I still find bits of plastic on the beach and I hear that there were more fish in the old days.

Our harbour gets annual visits from orca who come in to feed on stingrays, although in the eight years I've been here I've missed every visit.

Like many communities living by the coast, ours is taking action to reduce sewage overflow and run-off into our harbour, but there is still more to be done.

I've planted trees to filter the water that runs off my property into the harbour, and we have a sewerage system that treats all our waste and then pumps it out through into our orchard, so nothing from our waste goes down into the harbour.

Regenerating the sea

We're all familiar with the need to rewild the land, but what about the sea? There are moves to take this very seriously by putting lost wild species back in our oceans.

In Fiji giant clams were so heavily overfished that by the 1980s they were thought to be extinct locally. Australian clams were brought in to start a breeding programme and then their offspring were released on coral reefs across Fiji.

This example could be replicated around our oceans as a way of bringing back fish species that have become extinct in one area by transplanting them from somewhere else, or breeding them in captivity and then releasing them.

But human intervention can go horribly wrong. In 2017 plans were made to capture some of the 30 vaquita porpoises left in our oceans, put them in captivity to breed and then release them into the Gulf of California, where they would live happily ever after.

The vaquita had suffered a major population crash as a result of illegal catching of the totoaba fish. Flesh from the totoaba's swim bladder can fetch high prices in China and this has generated a vast illegal fishing industry. Unfortunately, gill nets designed to catch totoaba are also the

perfect size for trapping vaquitas, which become tangled and drown. The Mexican government has recently tightened its laws against illegal fishing but the rewards for totoaba catches are so high that there has been little respite.

When attempts were made to capture two vaquita for the breeding programme, one panicked and had to be immediately set free, and a second swiftly died of a stress-induced heart attack.

The idea of keeping wild animals in captivity also goes against the grain for many people who have worked hard to free them from sea aquariums around the world.

For many aquatic animals, captive breeding and rewilding are just not going to happen. We'll probably never see animals such as great white sharks, hammerheads or narwhals living and breeding in aquariums, then being released into the wild.

Here in New Zealand we very successfully take birds from endangered species, pop them on a predator-free island and let them breed. Unfortunately it's so much more complicated with marine animals.

Instead the top priority is to come down hard on the fisheries industry to reduce bycatch and to fish sustainably. This is proving very difficult in New Zealand, as the fishing industry fights every move made by our government in this area.

We could also increase the number of marine reserves and ocean sanctuaries, and patrol them so that they don't get fished.

Another area we could look at is replanting ocean plants that provide food and protection for many fish species. Many kelp forests around the world are under threat, mainly because of pollution and climate change.

Kelp form spectacular underwater forests that provide habitats for fish, clean the water and sequester carbon, but in Portugal, for example, these forests have disappeared. Now a project is being trialled where spores are collected from donor populations of kelp, placed in mesh bags and attached to rocky reefs where kelp used to grow in abundance. The hope is that the spores released from the bags will create new patches of forest.

One thing we can do to protect the Tasman Sea and the Pacific Ocean that surround us is to support local initiatives to stop overfishing, bottom trawling and bycatch by the fishing industry. Sign some petitions, people!

We can also encourage more marine reserves and ocean sanctuaries. And if you are a keen fisherman or woman, please fish carefully and humanely. Never take more fish or shellfish than you can eat and always leave plenty behind.

Humane fishing – how to do it right

Like many New Zealanders I was brought up in and around boats, and that involved lots of fishing. One of the nicest memories I have of my childhood was getting up early on a Sunday morning and going fishing with my dad, just the two of us. It is something we have done throughout my life and I still use the wonderful rod and reel he gave me on my fortieth birthday.

I still fish, but something has changed. Mainly I no longer believe, as my dad told me when I was a little girl, that fish feel no pain. I know they do.

I had a chat with Dr Culum Brown — a leading researcher in the field of fish cognition at Macquarie University in Sydney — and he confirmed that fish are sentient beings, which means they have the capacity to suffer. They also have friends.

Experiments show that groups of fish recognise each other, and they are effective at foraging together as well as recognising and avoiding

predators. So there are lots of good reasons for being able to recognise one another and having friendships.

'The fact that the fish go to join someone they recognise means they do have some kind of value associated with the fish they know, and there's some fish, particularly really social ones, who do suffer from separation anxiety so if you take them away from their mates, then they get anxious and their stress rates go up. Their stress receptors and chemicals in their body are exactly the same as ours,' says Culum.

His work has taken him around the world studying fish, after a childhood spent snorkelling around some of the most beautiful reefs in Southeast Asia. Culum's marine biology studies have revealed many facts that up-end the basis of our common understanding of fish.

His research has shown that even the smallest fish are capable of learning and can retain memories for months. Within schools of fish, there is often a strict social hierarchy, which can include forms of bullying. His work has also revealed that stingrays have especially good memories and can even distinguish days of the week.

He has become an advocate for the humane treatment of fish. His message applies to people like me — a recreational fisher.

'My main message is that fishing is like any other form of hunting and so you have to accept that there are consequences for your actions and that fish are sentient and feel pain. If you catch it you have to kill it as humanely and quickly as possible. If you do that, I don't have a problem.'

Many people haul up fish and throw them into a chilly bin, where they die slowly. Other people, me included, use an ikejime stick, which is a metal spike that you thrust into the fish's head slightly behind and above the eye, causing immediate brain death. But even that can go wrong.

'Sometimes it doesn't work and you end up inflicting even more pain, so to be double-sure it is best to cut its gills so that it bleeds out. That way the fish can't regain consciousness if you haven't put the ikejime spike in properly and they are unconscious when you cut their gills,' says Culum.

He also asks people not to catch and release fish, which he sees as a pastime where people are 'literally having fun at the expense of another animal'.

'I find it hard to justify but if you are going to do it then use things like barbless hooks or a circle hook so you can get the fish off the line really fast. They are now making knotless nets which won't graze the skin of the fish if you insist on hauling it out of the water.'

But if possible, don't haul it out of the water at all, he says.

'Once you graze a fish you remove the mucus that covers them and they are then really prone to infection, mostly like a fungal infection, and they're going to die from that if the stress doesn't kill them first.'

He also says that there's nothing to stop you taking a photo, but leave the fish in the water while you do because fishes' bodies aren't designed to cope with gravity.

'They are neutrally buoyant in the water, so their bodies don't cope with being out of the water at all.'

He also says that playing a fish, where you let them swim away then slowly reel them in multiple times, is cruel — 'get them in as fast as possible.'

Culum says humane treatment also needs to be applied to crayfish, crabs, octopus and squid. In the not-too-distant future it will be illegal to boil a crayfish alive — you'll have to refrigerate it first so that it loses consciousness before cooking.

New Zealand welfare guidelines

The Animal Welfare Act 1999 applies to all fish, including wild-caught fish from commercial fishing. It is an offence to ill-treat them or to kill them in a way that causes unreasonable or unnecessary pain or distress. All fish (bony or cartilaginous), octopus, squid, lobster or crayfish (including freshwater) are covered.

Details around how to ensure that the killing of animals does not cause unreasonable or unnecessary pain or distress is given in the codes of welfare.

Codes of welfare can be developed for farmed species and companion animals, but not for wild animals, which means they do not cover commercial fishing.

The National Animal Welfare Advisory Committee (NAWAC), which develops codes of welfare, is currently developing a code of welfare for farmed fish.

How to kill a fish humanely

Use an ikejime spike and make sure you position it correctly through the head, slightly behind and above the eye, causing immediate brain death.

If you have done it correctly the fins of the fish will flare and then the fish will relax and look dead. Sometimes, however, they can come back to life and be in a lot of pain if you haven't quite placed the spike in the right part of the brain.

To prevent this, after you have used the ikejime spike you can cut through the fish's gills to bleed it out and to make sure it is dead (fish have a main artery running between the gills that you can cut). There are guides online if you aren't sure.

If you're catching and releasing

- Don't pull the fish out of the water.

- If you do pull the fish out, wear rubber dishwashing gloves so you cause as little damage as possible to the mucus covering its skin. If you don't have gloves, use a damp cloth.

- If you're using a net to pull fish out of the water, find one that is fish-friendly and made of rubber rather than string.

- Use hooks that are easy to remove without causing damage to the fish.

- Don't play the fish by letting it run then hauling it back. Bring it in as quickly as you can to cause the least stress.

Antoinette's raw fish

---

*My first mother-in-law would make huge bowls of this salad ready
for when we arrived in Tauranga to visit. My kids love this and
have lovely memories of devouring it at Tauranga Grandma's table.
Antoinette was Tahitian so this recipe doesn't use coconut milk,
which makes it really lovely and light. She was also very fussy about
the fish — it had to be super-fresh and preferably snapper.*

*Antoinette used really tart lemons or preferably limes — you need that
to 'cook' the fish; sweet old lemons just won't do the trick. I never had this
recipe written down because Antionette just made it from memory. When
I asked her for it she recited it down the phone without many quantities.
This is my version — it's never as good as hers, but it's still delicious.*

1 kg fresh, fresh, fresh fish,
preferably snapper

6 tart lemons or limes

1 red capsicum

1 red onion

salt and pepper

Vinaigrette

¼ cup olive oil

2 tbsp malt vinegar

salt and pepper

To make the vinaigrette, whisk the olive oil into the malt vinegar until
it emulsifies. Add salt and pepper to taste.

Cut your fish up into bite-sized cubes. It helps to keep every piece
about the same size so the fish cooks evenly in the juice.

Squeeze your limes or lemons and pour the juice over the fish in a glass bowl (not a metal bowl). As you do this, squeeze the fish so that the juice is evenly distributed. When the juice just covers the fish, give it one last squeeze and set aside in the fridge for half an hour.

Meanwhile, chop up the capsicum and onion into tiny pieces, no bigger than your fingernail.

Check the fish to see if it is ready. It should be white and be fresh and tender to the taste.

Take handfuls of the fish and squeeze out as much of the juice as you can, then place it into another bowl. Add the capsicum and onion, then pour over the vinaigrette. Add salt and pepper to taste.

Brown butter fish

I mistakenly invented this dish after forgetting about my fish and coming back to find the butter all brown and the fish delicious. Now it is the only way I cook fish. It is fabulous for fish like kahawai and mullet, which seem to adapt to the brown butter flavour very well. Having said that, I'll cook pristine snapper this way too.

4 fillets lovely fish

salt and pepper

100 g butter

juice of 1 lemon

Place the fish fillets on a board and liberally sprinkle salt and pepper over both sides, rubbing it into the flesh.

Melt the butter in a heavy-based cast-iron pan or similar over a medium heat. If you have a large pan you may want to use more butter. When the butter is melted you'll need a big pool of butter sitting there.

The butter will start to bubble furiously and that is when you put your fish in. It should be swimming in hot butter. Keep the heat going and watch the butter slowly start to brown. The underside of your fish should be crisp and brown after about 5 minutes.

Turn the fish over as the butter continues to brown, and add the lemon juice over the fish and the butter. It will sizzle delightfully and you can spoon any excess brown butter over the fish.

The fish should be coated in lovely brown butter but also be quite crisp and golden. Serve immediately.

Rivers

In recent years attention has focused, quite rightly, on the state of our rivers. Fifteen New Zealand rivers have World Conservation Orders over them, which is the highest level of protection that can be afforded to any water body. It's like being a National Park, only it's a river.

This is a great start, but we have a long way to go. As I was researching the state of our rivers I pulled up a report from the Ministry for the Environment on the state of our waters in 2020 and was dismayed to see headings such as:

- 'Our native freshwater species and ecosystems are under threat'

- 'Water is polluted in urban, farming, and forestry areas'

- 'Changing water flows affect our freshwater'

- 'Climate change is affecting freshwater in Aotearoa'

The report brings together all available studies and is not a hopeful read. It points out that our waterways are under threat from pollution, from climate change, from the alteration of water courses for irrigation and electricity production, and from the conversion of land to cities and towns, farms and plantation forest (and associated pollution).

When I read a report like this I tend to skim through to the end where I look for a conclusion. You'll usually see a summary there: what hope there is, what will be done, and how these issues will be fixed.

In this report there was none of that. Instead there was a call for better reports, more information and an ability to put all that into a form that can be collated to make sense.

In other words, we can't act to protect our waterways until we have rigorous reporting to tell us what is actually happening.

My take from all this is that it's up to us. I am quite sure that in five years I will read the 2026 version of the same report and find that it's still a matter of needing more rigorous reporting.

Meanwhile, in the Hokianga where I live, I see local farmers fencing off streams and waterways to prevent their cattle polluting it. I see others, like me, planting heaps of native trees. I see new houses being built with sewerage systems like ours to reduce the load on the harbour.

It is really up to us, as it is with most things, to make a difference.

Estuaries

One person who spends a lot of time looking at our waterways is marine environmental scientist Dr Shari Gallop. Shari is a coastal environmental scientist and geomorphologist who studies estuaries.

Estuaries are shallow water bodies where rivers meet the sea. Most of the megacities around the world are based beside estuaries (like Tokyo, London and San Francisco). New Zealand has more than 300 estuaries, and many of our own cities are also built around them, such as Auckland, Tauranga and Christchurch. In the past, estuaries have been considered by some as 'low value' — meaning that some of them have been drained to make space for farmland. Generally, estuaries haven't been looked after as well as they should have been.

'Estuaries are really important,' says Shari. 'They are biodiversity hotspots, an important food source, and a transport link via ports. They are also a space for capturing carbon. Many people know that trees are important for capturing carbon, but so are estuaries. Estuaries capture carbon in their mangroves, saltmarsh, seagrass and sediments. This means less carbon dioxide in our atmosphere — a major greenhouse gas causing global warming. They are also nature's water filters — filtering water of sediments, nutrients and other pollutants. And they are culturally important, particularly for Māori. They have been (and are) a place to gather kaimoana (seafood), as well as a source of plants for rongoā (medicine) and for weaving. Additionally, estuaries are a place to share community and pass down intergenerational knowledge.'

Shari says that everybody can be a part of taking care of our environment and waterways.

'I think it's important to remember that we are part of our environment and everything is connected. In Te Ao Māori (the Māori world view), this is part of the concept of kaitiakitanga (guardianship) — which means people are part of our natural environment, we are connected by whakapapa to our environment and all the things in it, and should act as guardians. I think this is a good concept to use when thinking about how we can take care of our waterways.'

Here are some things you can do:

- Reduce consumption of single-use plastics and dispose of them correctly. Pick up any rubbish you see.

- Don't over-use fertilisers and other chemicals in gardens (as well as in agriculture/horticulture).

- Use environmentally-friendly cleaning products.

- Clean up dog poo so it doesn't wash into waterways.

- Use a car wash (they should have filters to remove chemicals) or wash your car on the lawn if you can — the soil can filter the dirt and soap rather than letting it wash into our waterways.

- If you go boating/fishing in freshwater lakes and rivers, ensure that you check, clean and dry your equipment to prevent spread of pests such as didymo ('rock snot').

- Plant more trees — too much sedimentation is a major problem for estuaries due to land clearance. Native vegetation along rivers and streams is especially important.

- Don't overfish — know the limits and stick to them, including for shellfish.

- Reduce pollution — use less plastics and dispose of them correctly. Don't pour harmful substances, like oil and paint, down the drain.

- Tell your local council if you see something that is not right, such as illegally dumped rubbish or pollution spills.

Ocean swimming

As Kiwis, I think we tend to take it for granted that our favourite beach in the summer will be there, crisp and perfect, whenever we need a swim. But we've also all seen signs warning people not to take seafood because it is contaminated or telling us not to swim because the bay is polluted. We should not accept this. We should demand that our local councils and regional authorities act to clean up that water.

Recently I've become very attuned to salt water, mainly because I've taken up ocean swimming.

In the eighties I lived at Opahi Bay in Mahurangi, north of Auckland. Every day an old guy — who was probably just in his late fifties, like I am now — would go swimming in the sea, rain or shine, winter or summer. At the time I thought he was barking mad. Now that person is me.

I first heard of ocean swimming from food writer Nici Wickes who, like me, lives near the sea and loves to get in it. Then a writer for my magazine *Thrive* pitched a story about it to me. Once I read that story, I was sold. The benefits seemed to be enormous and there was nothing stopping me except a nagging feeling I would get cold.

I took my first ocean swim in January 2021 but only after I had bought a long-sleeved rash vest swimsuit with a cool zip down the front so I didn't have to keep putting on sunscreen. And a new pair of really expensive goggles. And a new waterproof watch that could time me — it says 'Ironman' on it so it makes me feel extra athletic. And a float that you tow behind you so that jet-skis don't run you over — also, if you get tired, you can hold on to it and float around for a while. I think that is why my physiotherapist suggested I buy one. I have never used this float but it was an important part of the equipment-gathering process that precedes all exercise fads. We all get the yoga gear, the yoga mat, the roly thing and lots of other necessary yoga stuff before we actually do a yoga session.

Once I had all my equipment I walked down the paddock ready to take the first plunge at high tide.

Billie, our young cow, got terribly excited about seeing me in my swim gear. It may have been that the rash vest had a bright pattern on it, or that I was clutching my goggles in my hand so she thought they were a treat I had forgotten to give her. All I know is that Billie wanted

to play, which is quite a thing with a 400-kg cow. Cows play a lot like dogs. So Billie would run at me full tilt, which could be interpreted as a charging action in a bull fight by those who don't know cows. She would then pull up to a stop only when her head was about to hit my chest. I would put my hand up in a desperate 'stop now!' motion, which seemed to signal to her that it was fine to run away and charge all over again. What a great game she had discovered.

She did this ten times as I slowly inched my way down the paddock. I love Billie, and I understand that cows play, but when they're that big it is very unnerving and you don't want to turn your back on them for a minute. So I was basically walking backwards, throwing my stop-now hands out and fearing for my life.

Finally I reached the gate and found safety on the other side. The dogs joined me from the neighbouring property where they had been sheltering behind the fence from Billie's games.

Slightly grumpy, I made my way down to the beach and just plunged in after putting my goggles on and setting my watch. My aim was to do 20 minutes. I managed 5 minutes out into the Hokianga Harbour before I realised that it was really deep and the further out I went, the stronger the outgoing current was getting. So I swam back in.

Originally my aim was to reach Mahena Island, which is just off the beach. It's a little island that I thought would be lovely to reach, sit on the bit of sand on the leeward side and then swim back. I was possibly also imagining pointing it out to friends and telling them I swam to it every day as a way to impress them.

But the currents scared me. I've been in and around the sea long enough to respect it. So the next day I swam horizontally along the bay, keeping in line with the coast. This was much better, except that I swam into a few boulders on the beach that get covered up by the high tide and I ripped open my hand on an oyster shell.

The dogs swam with me on the first swim. Both are water-loving dogs and good swimmers and must have thought this was a lot of fun.

The next day, however, they swam out a little way, then headed back and opted to wait on the beach while keeping a sharp eye on me at all times. Now they walk along the beach keeping pace with me in the water, and when I'm finished and I call them out to me, I throw a ball or stick or whatever they bring me. They enjoy playing fetch in the water. Getting them swimming is really good exercise, especially for Rosie, who is getting older and shouldn't do anything too stressful on her joints.

That first day wasn't the best start to my ocean swimming career. The next day I put up a solar-powered electric fence in the paddock, which gave me a safe walkway free of Billie's charges. The last thing I needed was an anxious start to my swims.

Thanks to my dad, who was a champion swimmer in his youth and a good swimming teacher, I am a very natural, easy swimmer. The actual swimming part of ocean swimming was of no concern.

Finally, after much trial and error I settled on a span of the beach where I had figured out which rocks were where at low tide. It gives me a clear run at high tide or two hours either side (or three hours if there is a full moon and a higher than usual tide). I swim 10 minutes up and 10 minutes back. Sometimes if it is quite rough it can be 10 minutes up and 20 minutes back if I have to battle the tide and big waves. And I never go deeper than I can stand so that should the orcas turn up I can run to safety.

I would be lying if I didn't admit that those first few weeks in the ocean were a bit terrifying. A girl had just been killed by a shark down the coast at Waihi Beach and I knew that at certain times our bay is littered with stingrays. I really felt that I was venturing into someone else's world, which is absolutely true.

But eventually I got used to this world and realised that sharks don't often hunt in a harbour, the orcas were unlikely to come into the shallows where I was swimming, and I just needed to be careful where I placed my feet getting in and out of the water to avoid the stingrays, who really would rather not have anything to do with me and are very unlikely to sting me if I just leave them alone.

As the weather cooled, so did the ocean. I'm not going to lie to you, it's bloody freezing.

The first day I realised that things were getting a bit chilly was when my face froze. As I swam I could feel every nerve in my face paralysed into inaction. I couldn't have smiled if I'd wanted to — I imagine that is how women feel when they get Botox.

It wasn't a very nice feeling and I very nearly ditched the swim and headed home to a hot bath.

But then I realised that somewhere in the world, possibly even in New Zealand, at some very expensive spa, was a very rich woman spending a lot of money to have blocks of salt-water ice rubbed all over her face in what was probably called an Anti-Ageing Bionic Skin Refresher. The only difference between us was that she was probably reclining gracefully in a luxurious bathrobe while I was splashing about in my onesie.

So I persisted, the frozen face adjusted and I got on with my swim and ended it smiling, a lot.

A few weeks later I was at a party, which is almost unheard of in my life these days. I was boring someone with my ocean swimming stories when they pointed out a very beautiful older woman across the room and said she was an ocean swimmer too.

I got close enough to take a good look at her and oh, her skin! I was looking at a face that was smooth and gently flushed with the reminder of youth.

So I persisted with the cold ocean swimming, but if I'm honest I didn't do it quite as often as in the warmer months.

Where I live, the coolest water temperature is 14°C in the middle of winter, which is nothing compared with the ocean swimmers in the northern hemisphere who swim in minus 5°C water. I also have a wetsuit that I put on for those winter swims.

Some people see cold water as a wonder cure for everything that ails you. According to the Dutch 'Ice Man', Wim Hof, immersion in cold water can do everything from improving our bodies' natural recovery process to relieving symptoms of various medical conditions and can even help weight loss.

Wim Hof is the reason you see men on social media leaping into buckets of ice. I say men because it's mostly men who do it. Women, like me, just hop in the ocean and quietly freeze. We don't like a fuss.

Some people talk of getting a shot of adrenaline from the shock of the cold water and having a super-amazing out-of-body cool-mind thing happen, but I've never had that.

But I have found myself saying out loud, on several occasions, 'Thank you sea for being here.' It came as a complete shock the first time it happened but now I just see it as my own version of an involuntary super-amazing out-of-body cool-mind thing.

I do get a lovely, cosy, warm, almost tingly feeling when I'm back at the house, dried off and dressed. It's a nice afterglow.

One of the benefits of ocean swimming for me is that it's a very meditative process. The repetition of the strokes combined with the regular breathing puts you in a very relaxed state. I find that it opens up my creativity, similar to going for a long walk or meditating.

Another benefit is that I find the sea water incredibly soothing. You are buoyant and the water strokes you as you swim.

Salt water is full of minerals we need for our body, especially magnesium, which can be absorbed through your skin and is good for healthy bones, muscles and nerves. It is especially good for the skin, leaving it smooth and supple. The salt water also detoxifies my skin as I swim. And it stimulates blood circulation, which is possibly why when I swim regularly I notice my blood pressure drops.

But the best benefit is that my body is getting a really good workout without placing any pressure on my joints, as it would if I was running. I have had one knee replacement and I've got another to come, so running is out for me, but swimming is totally doable. When I finish I don't feel especially exhausted, probably because of the way I breathe — I don't feel hot and sweaty, and it's only a few hours later that I feel like I've had a workout.

An ocean swim leaves me feeling fantastic for the rest of the day. I also like the fact that it's not something prescriptive like going to the gym three times a week at the same time. I swim when the tide is right, so some days I don't swim at all because it is too early or too late, and sometimes I swim every day for a week while the high tide is happening during the day. It feels like I am connected with nature and that is all good for me.

I only swim for 20 minutes and have resisted the need to keep adding 5 minutes more until I can do an hour. I'm not in training for a triathlon, I'm just getting some exercise, so 20 minutes is enough, no need to get adventurous. Sometimes I swim longer if I'm really enjoying it but most days 20 minutes is about right.

Homemade salt

---

*If you're visiting the beach, you might like to take a bucket of sea
water home and have a go at making your own sea salt.*

Pour a bucket of clean sea water into a big pot and boil, uncovered,
until you have a slurry at the bottom — this takes about 2 hours.

Place that slurry in a large roasting pan and put it outside when you
know you are going to have some hot, dry weather. After three to four
days in direct sun you will have about a cup of salt to enjoy and give a
trendy name to. Hokianga Harbour sea salt, anyone?

Do check that the place you are gathering your sea water from is
not polluted.

Animals and us

When you fall in love with an animal it's a lovely thing. Your world is automatically upgraded to one where you have an extra special spark in your day, a little being who constantly reminds you how wonderful the world is, how lovely love is and how gorgeous a cuddle can be on a sad day.

The love of an animal is unconditional and constant, something we all need in our lives. We tend to think of ourselves as carers of our animals, but I believe they are our carers as well.

At the moment in the Hokianga we have three cats — Peggy, Dickie and Sassy — all strays who found their way into our lives. Peggy only has three legs after being found in a hedge with a badly mauled hind leg. She started off by living with us but, as cats do, she decided she liked my father better and now lives with him in his cottage.

He loves her, spoils her and is fascinated by her. My dad adores animals and I think Peggy gives him the company he needs and something to fuss over. In return she'll reward him with a range of weird behaviours that keep him entertained. We're pretty sure Peggy was a wild kitten because she's not at all cuddly and barely tolerates being stroked. She's small, calico-coloured and very beautiful so she can get away with anything.

Sassy, at the grand old age of 18, has a hyperactive thyroid so she is very skinny and eats ravenously all day.

When our daughter Pearl, her main keeper, moved to Wellington we brought Sassy and her sister Lucy up to live with us. They had both been found in a sack on the side of the road as kittens and someone had attempted to cut Lucy's throat. The local vet gave them to us and the two of them lived happily growing up with our children, curling up like yin and yang. Lucy didn't like men very much.

Lucy didn't last long after her move to the country but made it to 17, and is buried under one of my rose bushes.

Sassy meows constantly for food and when she's not doing this, she is sleeping, as befits an old lady of her age. She especially likes Paul so when he sits down she will be on his lap within seconds.

Dickie turned up as a malnourished kitten on our deck one day and I slowly fed him and tamed him over three weeks. When he finally let me pat him I realised that he had been loved by someone else because he leaned in. He knew what it was like to be stroked and cuddled, possibly by a child nearby.

Where we live it is common for kittens to be dumped, because people can't afford to get their cats spayed.

Dickie has grown into a big, cuddly boy but he is plagued by a gum disease brought on by his period of malnutrition, so every few years he gets a few more teeth taken out. He will probably be toothless one day, but apparently cats cope okay with that. He is also a great mouser and the cuddliest cat we've ever owned.

My love of cats comes from my first childhood cat, Pizza. I have always had a cat and I like how individual and strong-willed cats are. They do as they please, but they also please us.

Our dogs Flo, a labradoodle, and Rosie, a huntaway cross, are our constant companions. We bought Rosie for 30 dollars out of the back of a van in the KFC carpark in Thames about eight years ago. She is a loyal dog who never leaves our sight, never wanders and hates thunder. She would have made a terrible farm dog.

Flo is more adventurous. She likes to wander, but not too far, prefers to spend her time outside and is never without a tennis ball in her mouth.

Both dogs are great fetchers and have a wonderful sense of smell. I once trained Flo to seek and find nests of chicken eggs around the property and she caught on really quickly. The only problem was that she would pick up an egg, then promptly drop it on the ground in front of me, as she does with a tennis ball. I decided it was better to have unbroken eggs than to find all the nests.

Both dogs give us cuddles all day long. They sleep on the floor in our bedroom, are occasionally allowed up on the beds and couches and are great guard dogs.

When we are away they move over to Dad's place and he loves the security of having them with him.

Even though our dogs have the run of our property, we still take them for a walk along the beach every day. This is a very mutual daily ritual. The dogs get to run, swim and sniff and we get to reap the benefits of being in nature.

I think dogs make great companions. They can also be great carers when needed for the disabled and the elderly.

For three years we had cows. Don't ask me why. Neither of us was raised on a farm or had any idea how to care for a cow.

One day I had the brilliant idea that we could get two calves on our two-acre paddock. They could be pets and also keep the grass down, living out their days in the sunshine.

So we bought Bruce, a black and white steer, and Bambi, a beautiful red cow, from the people who had been grazing them on our paddock. They were about a year old. We knew them well, they were quite tame and as I've written in my other books I would play games with them, throwing a blow-up exercise ball at them to have it headbutted back. I would lie down in the sun with them and have a snooze. They became my pets, with just as much character and intelligence as my dogs.

I loved stroking them and cuddling them and all was going well until they both became escape artists.

Bambi could easily unhook the clasp on our gate with her tongue and would let the pair of them into our garden and orchard, no trouble at all. I had read in *The Secret Life of Cows* by Rosamund Young about a cow who would let herself into the hay shed every night by doing exactly what Bambi was doing. But Rosamund's cow was even more clever than Bambi. She would unhook the gate and feast all night, but then re-hook the gate and get back in her paddock by the morning.

I was telling my farmer friend Pauline about this and she told me she used to have a cow who always found her way to the next paddock from the one her herd was in. Every day, Pauline would put her back, and every morning, there the cow would be on the other side.

I got a new gate hook that defied Bambi's tongue and thought that would be the end of the escaping. But then Bruce grew really big. I wasn't prepared for this because in New Zealand we rarely see a cow that is more than two years old.

My neighbour pointed out that Bruce could well grow to weigh a tonne. I laughed my head off until I hit Google and had it confirmed. When you're next driving in the country, keep an eye out for the prize bull most farmers keep on their properties, then think of a rhinoceros because that's what they look like. All muscle and grunt.

Bruce's size meant that he could simply push over our old fences any time he liked and escape into my neighbours' properties with Bambi in tow. The two of them could do a lot of damage in a very short time, and it also meant that Paul and I and usually Pauline had to spend the better part of an hour getting them back in.

I bought electric fences, I patched the fence we had and then on New Year's Day 2020 Bruce managed to push the whole fence down on one side and was raiding the neighbour's orchard as they watched horrified from their deck.

I had just had my knee op so was unable to do any wrangling, but it took 10 neighbours the best part of New Year's morning to get them back in the paddock. We felt awful, even though everyone reassured us they had nothing else to do, which was obviously a lie.

Paul came up with the idea of turning Bruce and Bambi, my pets, into homekill. This was the worst possible scenario for someone who just wanted to play with her pet cows for the next 20 years. But they had to go; we couldn't keep relying on the goodwill of our neighbours. We had to be responsible cow owners.

I won't go into the details but we ended up with two freezers full of meat. I couldn't eat it but Paul and most of our kids loved it, not to mention our friends.

When I finally got over my sulking and my grief and tried the meat,

I really couldn't believe how good it tasted, possibly because for the last few months of their lives Bruce and Bambi had had their diets supplemented with a bucket of feijoas from our trees most days. Not to mention a million other treats I had been feeding them.

I also knew that unlike the meat we get from the supermarkets, my cows had never been terrified by being loaded on to a truck then driven to the freezing works where all sorts of inhumane things would happen to them. They had never known a day's stress in their life apart from being herded home from the neighbours' properties.

We also know that the meat from our cows was more nutritious than the meat you can buy in the supermarkets. Thanks to Isabella Tree's research for her book on rewilding, we know that chemical analysis of wild-fed beef grazed entirely on pasture shows far higher levels of vitamins A and E and usually double the levels of beta-carotene (the precursor of vitamin A) and selenium — all powerful antioxidants.

It also contains higher levels of healthy fatty acids, including the long-chain omega-3 fatty acid DHA, which protects against heart disease and plays a key role in brain function and development. It also has higher levels of conjugate acid (CLA), a fatty acid with proven benefits for the immune and inflammatory system as well as bone mass. Considered to be one of the most powerful anti-carcinogens in nature, CLA is also proven to reduce body fat and the risk of heart attack.

It appears that humans find it easier to metabolise fat from animals that are grass-fed. Eating grain-fed animal fat can be detrimental to human health, with increasing evidence of links to obesity, cardiovascular disease, diabetes, asthma, autoimmune disease and cancers, as well as depression, ADHD and Alzheimer's. As Isabella points out, we don't need to cut animal fats from our diet — we should simply take care to eat the right sort of animal fat.

In New Zealand most of our meat is pasture-fed, but there are some farmers who feed grain. As a consumer we may not know which we are eating when we pick up that pack of meat in the supermarket chiller.

Globally around a third of all grain produced is fed to livestock. Over the past 15 years, 5.5 million hectares of pasture land has been ploughed up in Europe mainly for growing grain to feed livestock.

I don't eat a lot of meat these days, but when I do I would much rather eat it from a cow I raised in the sunshine on my paddock who never had a moment's stress, than meat sourced from the meatworks.

AFTER BAMBI AND BRUCE were gone I sulked for a few months, then Paul decided he'd quite like to do it all over again, which is when we bought wee Betty from Pauline.

I agreed to let Paul raise cows for meat, but I said I wanted nothing to do with it. I would not raise pets to be killed again.

But when Betty arrived she was a poor sick calf who had been pushed off the teat by her twin. She was smaller than our dogs. I fed her twice a day for weeks with buckets of warm calf-milk formula, which smelled like vanilla milkshakes. She slowly got a bit better and started growing. When Billie, the rudely healthy calf, joined her in the paddock I thought my worrying days were over. But no.

Betty would look at me every day with doleful eyes that sent me the message: I am a runt, that is what I am and always will be. I'm so sorry about that.

She wasn't thriving and had a terrible cough. The vet sent me some medicine that involved two injections and a drench. There was no way I could do this on my own, so with the help of Pauline and Paul I tied Betty to the fence then somehow managed to sandwich myself between Betty, the fence and the gate in an effort to keep her enclosed so that we could give her the injections. So much for raising a cow with no stress.

Once that was achieved and Betty and I were so tightly enclosed that neither of us could really breathe, Pauline started sneezing and needed to blow her nose. I wondered how this would all end. Would Betty, who weighs 150 kg, kick her way clear of me and the gate, killing me in the process? Or would we both just squeeze each other to death? In the end Pauline stopped sneezing and rammed one injection into Betty's bum and one in her neck, and I managed to shove a drench down Betty's throat.

Betty rallied a bit but she was still giving me the runt look, which I was starting to think was down to a bad attitude. So I fed her treats and tonics and played her Mozart on my phone. She wouldn't come near me any more after the injection episode, which was understandable.

Betty was plagued by illness all her life. She continued to cough constantly, was lethargic and then developed a huge abscess on the side of her face that just wouldn't clear up.

It didn't help that her paddock-mate, Billie, who was the same age, was twice her size, rudely healthy and quite the perfect cow both in temperament and vitality. Everyone who saw her and knew about cattle admired her and told me she could win prizes at A&P shows. Meanwhile, Betty would stand by, head dropped, coughing constantly and occasionally nibbling slowly on a blade of grass. The time came to call it, and let Betty go. She'd had a good life at our place by the sea, and we just didn't see the point in letting it drag on.

We're not strangers to putting animals down since we moved to the country. There are about 10 chickens at the bottom of my vege patch — hens who got sick, young roosters that needed to go — all killed by Paul, who seems to be able to manage it without getting upset. Next to them are possums I've trapped in our orchard and the carcasses of fish I have caught.

Despite this, I found I simply could not adjust to this side of country living. I know that some of you will feel the same as me, but in the country you need to harden up or else it's going to be tough.

When the man with the gun arrived, I begged him to wait until I'd driven far away before he did the deed. I heard the shot just as I was getting into the car. What followed was hyperventilating, wanting to throw up and tears flowing down my face as I drove off. No matter how much I told myself it was for the best, I was still completely rattled by the death of one of our animals. Meanwhile, Billie apparently continued eating her feijoa and apple treats and seemed to cope quite well without her friend.

And so, after a few years of country living where I delighted in caring for our livestock, I decided to call time on that for my mental health. If you're someone who lives with anxiety, then it makes sense to find what drives it and remove it from your life if you can.

Having been concerned about Betty for more than a year, I no longer had to worry every time I heard her cough. That just left Billie.

I sat Paul down and said I didn't feel up to being a farmer in that sense. Chickens I can do, but cows for meat I can't. We agreed that once Billie was gone, that would be the end of our cows and we would regenerate the paddock into native bush. It felt like the right thing to do.

A few months later we put some calves owned by my neighbour in the paddock to help Billie keep the grass down, and I realised that Billie hadn't actually been that happy on her own.

When she saw them from across the paddock she let out a moo that was more a screech of delight. It's hard to describe because I'd never heard anything like it before or since. She then came running down to greet the calves and immediately sought out an older calf called Wiremu, who she coaxed into having a game of headbutt then chase around the paddock, just as she had been trying to do with me on my ocean swim treks through the paddock down to the beach.

Within seconds she was happily ensconced with Wiremu and Garry, the older steers. I realised that cows are herd animals and it's very unfair not to give them mates.

I watched Billie for a few months and then I realised that she too would go the way of the gun because the meat in the freezer was getting low and Paul was making noises about Billie's time being near.

When Pauline came to retrieve her calves, there was no way Billie was remaining behind on her own so she trotted off with them happily to live over on Pauline's paddocks until the man with the gun turned up.

When this happened I had a terrible day of sadness, which was helped just a little bit by the knowledge that this would never happen again. Despite this happening to millions of cows all over New Zealand on a regular basis, I would not be part of it any more.

Animals like us

As a city girl, my love of animals is a bit surprising. We had one family cat and one poodle when I was growing up, but somewhere in my Danish, Norwegian and British DNA is a definite love of having animals close by.

Studies show that being around animals is great for your bacterial biodiversity. Getting a good lick from a dog or a cow every day is very beneficial. The physical act of cuddling an animal is also good for you, especially if you are living alone.

But I think what I like most about animals is the way they behave. I can sit and watch any animal for hours, just to marvel at how they communicate with their friends, the fact that they can be complete clowns at times and how much time they spend grooming themselves. One of my favourite things to watch is a cat cleaning its face. Very cute.

I read a story in *The Times* about some dolphins at the Marine Life Oceanarium in Gulfport, Mississippi, where litter found its way to the

bottom of their pool. Fishing it out was difficult so the staff decided to save themselves some work by training the dolphins to do it for them. Each time a dolphin dived down and brought up a crisp packet or a drinks can, it was rewarded with a fish.

At some point, the trainers noticed that one dolphin was doing a lot better than the others. Kelly was getting a lot more fish. Odder still, her scraps of rubbish were smaller than the other dolphins'. They investigated. Kelly, it turned out, was playing them. When Kelly found a piece of litter, she hid it under a rock at the bottom of the pool. Then when she was hungry, she tore off a bit and traded it for a fish. In this way she turned one fish into many.

There are many other stories like this, including Santino the chimpanzee who stores rocks in a pile during the night then flings them at visitors to the zoo in the day. There's Inky the octopus who escaped his aquarium and reached the Pacific Ocean. There's the crows that have learned to drop nuts on a zebra crossing, using the passing cars as automotive nutcrackers.

These stories are evidence that animals are incredibly intelligent, but do we also like that they are a bit like us?

'Maybe we feel closer to other animals when we see them behaving in ways that we do,' Peter Singer, professor of bioethics at Princeton University, told *The Times*. 'It shows that there's not this huge gulf. It's not that all humans are over here, and we have these rights and deserve this respect, and then there's the animals in some other huge category.'

As I wrote that last sentence I could hear Rosie the huntaway letting out a very delicate whine. I looked across from the kitchen table where I was typing and she was sitting by the couch looking at me hopefully. I have trained my dogs to ask first before they hop up on the couch or bed, and this is what she was doing. I don't blame her: the fire is roaring, it's a rare 5°C outside and she has the right idea — take it easy.

I spend hours watching my animals and learning from them. Rosie had been on a walk, and now it was rest time. That's something else I can learn from her — how to rest.

Every day around midday all my chickens retire to the bush to have their dust baths, sunbathe and nod off. Sometimes I find Tonga, the head rooster, on his own in a quiet place gently nodding off, a relief from those annoying chickens.

I like to sit and watch my chickens, mostly in the evening when I feed them. We have 24 chickens now and it's an opportunity for me to check that they are all healthy and then sit back and laugh at their bickering. There is a definite pecking order with hens, and just spending 10 minutes with my chickens can tell you who is top and who is bottom. This can also change if a dominant hen is moulting and looks like shit — she will often be demoted and only allowed back into her old position once she looks better. If a chicken is sick she will swiftly fall down the pecking order, and that's when I'll notice something is wrong with her.

After they've been fed they'll usually wander off to a sunny spot and have a good groom before taking off for a last-minute forage prior to bedtime. They don't sleep in a hen house because my chickens are what I call 'wildly free-range'.

Wildly free-range

This is a way of keeping chickens that I like to think I've invented, but I'm sure there are many people around the country doing the same or a similar thing.

I realised that I was keeping chickens in a new way when some friends came to stay and told me they were going to start raising organic chickens to sell for meat. My friend said to her husband: 'Go and look at

Wendyl's operation. Her chickens seem very healthy and fat!'

He walked up the driveway with me and then I pointed at a big ngaio tree and said 'That's the operation, right there. One tree. It's a ngaio, where they go nigh nigh at night.'

He glanced up politely and I could tell he thought I had consumed too many wines.

I then pointed at a rubbish bin and said 'That's the other part of the operation — good-quality feed.'

I reached in and grabbed a handful of barley, oats, sunflower seeds, peas, wheat and corn seeds. No extruded pellets for my birds.

To his credit he didn't laugh, but he's a beef farmer and I know he was expecting some expansive hen house with all the mod cons.

I pointed to the ngaio because that's where my chickens sleep. They don't sleep in the hen house I had built for them, nor do they lay in the nest boxes. Instead they spend all day roaming outside, digging for worms and bugs, eating seeds, having dust baths and sunbathing, then one by one they climb up that tree to the branch they always perch on and go to sleep. There is a strict order here too, with the most dominant sleeping at the top. Every hen goes to her own branch every night.

I think they like the ngaio because a second group of hens, protected by my other rooster, Max, sleep in another ngaio tree by the driveway. Māori would use the leaves of the ngaio tree to repel mosquitos, so perhaps there's something in that and it allows the hens to keep mites and bites away.

As for sleeping in trees, this is what chickens do in the wild. Domestic chickens were bred from the Southeast Asian red junglefowl around 8000 years ago, and red junglefowl sleep high up in the trees at night.

I only have two chickens who don't sleep in a tree, and they were saved from a battery farm. The only thing they have ever known is sleeping in a box, so the two of them snuggle up in the nest boxes my dad built for the hens to lay their eggs in. These two hens then proceed to fill the boxes full of poo every night, which means I am constantly cleaning them out and no hen in her right mind will lay an egg in there.

My chickens are much safer in the ngaio at night because if they were shut up in a hen house and a predator like a stoat or wild cat got in, there would be nowhere for them to go. In a tree they can peck below them and push and fly higher if they need to. I think they at least have a fighting chance.

Chickens cannot see well at night, so I try to keep away from their tree as the sun goes down or else my presence can set everyone off in an alarming chorus of danger.

The other nice thing about chickens roosting in trees is that all their droppings land on the ground and are widely spread, unlike droppings in a hen house that they walk in, feed by and sit in.

They are also not crammed in together, nor are they shut in a house. This means that disease and mites don't have a chance to spread, or find a nice warm place to multiply.

Combine this with their daily dust baths, which not only keep them clean but also take some excess oil off their feathers, and my hens are very clean and hygienic.

Sometimes when it's freezing outside and hailing hard I have a pang of guilt that my hens are in the tree and they are getting soaked, but they all seem to survive it. Their feathers are coated in oil and act much like an umbrella. Hens don't like being in the rain during the day and will always seek shelter, but if you watch one in a downpour the water just pours off them.

I also think that withstanding inclement weather and cold toughens them up. They are built to withstand these conditions because they are wild animals. Since I gave up trying to herd them into their hen house every night they have not had one single illness, no mites, no worms in five years. I've also not lost a hen to a predator, which is pretty amazing out here in the country. Something is working.

Once a week I scoop up all the droppings under the tree into a wheelbarrow and deposit them on my lovely compost.

Wild feeding

I watch what I feed my hens. A lot of chook feed you can buy commercially has grains that have been imported and therefore treated to prevent bugs and other things coming into the country.

Grain intended for the consumption of birds and animals is irradiated at a dose of 25 kGy (kilogray) to kill parasites and bacterial, fungal and viral pathogens. This is about the same dosage used to sterilise medical equipment.

I understand why this is done, but this treatment is not advised for food to be consumed by humans — yet my hens would eat the grain and then I would eat their eggs.

An Australian Government report acknowledges that gamma radiation can have effects on certain vitamins and other nutrients, and it produces peroxides and other radiolytic by-products, some of which may be toxic or carcinogenic. It then goes on to quote studies from the sixties showing that carbohydrates, proteins and fats are fine after radiation, it's 'just' the micronutrients that can be affected.

If the grain and seed isn't irradiated it is heat-treated, which also kills off valuable nutrients.

In keeping with my efforts to grow nutrient-rich food to nourish myself, I am also interested in getting nutrient-rich eggs out of my chickens. I don't think that feeding them radiated grains and seeds is going to be a good thing for that.

It took me a while but eventually I found a chicken food that featured New-Zealand-grown grains and seeds, which meant they didn't need to be irradiated.

The feed is made by Topflite and is all grown in Oamaru. Its ingredients are self-evident when you open the bag. There are whole sunflower seeds, corn, barley wheat, oats and green peas staring right at you. These are the first to go when the chickens start feeding. There are also poultry pellets that have added vitamins and minerals.

Supa Feeds is another brand that uses local grain, but it is a textured feed, which means you can't see all those homegrown seeds when you open the bag. Nor do the hens get the complete article to digest themselves, which is what they would do in the wild.

My Topflite chicken feed costs $39 for 20 kg on special, which is more than other feeds. But I reason that I am getting the benefit of those extra dollars in the nutrient level of my eggs.

In winter I feed my hens twice a day, usually about half a cup per hen, per day. In summer they get fed once a day. This is because in summer there are grasses, native trees and weeds growing with plenty of seeds and berries they can eat, as well as fallen fruit in the orchard. In the dead of winter it can be harder to find those extra treats.

I also feed my hens a lot of scraps, such as milk and yoghurt that has seen better days, leftover dinner and stale bread.

I also add a splash of homemade apple cider vinegar daily into their main water bowls to give them extra nutrition and protection from bugs.

The key to a healthy hen, I think, is diversity of diet, just like it is for us. Recently I added to their food supply by planting a row of 15 native mingimingi bushes, which not only provide valuable coverage for hens to hide under from predators like hawks, but also produce masses of blue berries at hen height for them to feed on.

Wild eggs

One of the downsides of 'wildly free-range' is that you will not find your eggs laid in neatly arranged nests. I'm fine with that because there is nothing natural about a chicken climbing a little ladder into a little house to lay her eggs in a prescribed nest box measured out to a precise size.

What hens really like is to lay eggs in a nest they have made somewhere quiet and dark and hidden. So that's what my hens do. They find just the right place, sometimes at the base of a flax bush, sometimes on a pile of wood, sometimes under the house under an old rangehood, sometimes in an agapanthus bush. When one hen has found a new spot, all the others want to lay there too. It's the new cool place. Usually I find the new nest because one hen will be making a hell of a racket right next to it, trying to make the hen that is laying its egg get off the nest so that she can lay hers. This can go on all morning as they all line up to lay in the best new place in town.

I can also spot a nest by simply following a hen who has taken off from her breakfast in a hell of a hurry, looking for all the world like she really needs to take a dump. It can sometimes be a bit hard to keep up, but if you do you can follow her to the nest and go back later, when you will find quite a few eggs.

Sometimes you'll miss a nest, then one day you'll be pulling out some wood for the fire or poking about in a bush and you'll find 30 eggs. Just put them in a bucket half-filled with water; those that float are no good, and the others you should eat quite quickly.

The good thing about the nests your hens choose is that they will often go back to them when no one has laid there for weeks. On our property we have about ten nest sites we keep an eye on and they all have names.

One is called the Happy House because it is just a small old hen house the size of a dog kennel we used temporarily to house a mother and her chicks to stop a wild cat killing them. Once we took the run off it we found that the hens loved to lay in it, so we shifted it just around from the kitchen and it is reliably always full of eggs at the end of the day. We also have an old camping safe that they love called the Camp Nest. There is a nest under the house by the pump, so that's called the Pump Nest. You get the idea.

The best thing about these nests is that they are just used for laying and a hen will never shit in her own nest. They remain really clean and only require the occasional straw replacement, although we tend to leave them to self-clean with rain and wind. To me it is much healthier than keeping our hens all crammed in together in a house full of nest boxes where they also sleep and eat.

Best frittata ever

I make a lot of frittata to use up eggs when we have too many. Frittata can sometimes be a little dry and not that appetising. This won't happen with this recipe. The secret is to use cream, not milk.

olive oil

1 cup mushrooms, sliced

8 spears asparagus (if it's spring)

1 bunch spinach, chopped (about 8 leaves, including the stems)

2 cups grated cheddar cheese (I use Tasty)

8 eggs

½ cup cream

salt and pepper, to season

In an oven-proof frying pan — preferably cast-iron — heat the olive oil then fry the mushrooms and asparagus if you have it. When they are nearly cooked, add the chopped spinach and let it wilt.

When the veges look cooked, sprinkle over the grated cheese. Whisk together the eggs and cream, add some salt and pepper and pour that over everything. Let it cook for a minute.

Place under the oven grill on high for 5–10 minutes until it is fluffy and golden on top.

Prawn omelette

When I was 18 I worked as a waitress at the Hungry Horse restaurant in Elliot Street, central Auckland. I was a poor student working nights to pay my rent and I wasn't eating well. We were allowed to choose a staff meal and every night I chose the prawn omelette and devoured it. I make this omelette mainly because it brings back one of my first joyous food memories, but also because it's delicious.

1 cup raw prawn meat — no tails here

2 tsp sweet chilli sauce (see Paul's recipe on page 130)

3 large eggs

salt and pepper, to season

olive oil

¼ cup grated cheddar cheese

Mix the raw prawns with the sweet chilli sauce in a bowl and leave to marinate for 10 minutes.

In a separate bowl, whisk the eggs and add a bit of salt and pepper.

In a good frying pan heat up some olive oil and fry the prawns until they are pink and covered in chilli.

In another pan heat up some olive oil over a high heat. When the oil is smoking, pour in the eggs. Turn down the heat so the omelette will brown on the bottom but also cook through.

When the surface of the omelette is set, add the cooked prawns on one half of the omelette and sprinkle with the grated cheese. Gently pick up half of the omelette and fold it over the prawns and cheese. Leave to settle and set for a minute, then serve immediately.

Wild mothers

When your hens are not contained, it means that they are free to go and hatch some babies whenever and wherever they like. If one of our broody hens sits on a batch of eggs, we remove them every day until she gets sick of it and moves off the nest. This works well for the nests we know about. But every summer one or two of our broody hens make a nest in the bush, or in one case under an old rangehood under the house, and sits on the eggs.

Every summer we'll be feeding the chickens and suddenly a long-lost hen who we thought had been taken by a dog will turn up with a clutch of chicks. She always looks exhausted and we act quickly. We need to catch the mum and her babies and put them in a run so they are protected from wild cats and stoats. Otherwise every day we come out and there's one less chick.

Last summer our part-bantam, Top Knot, who one day just turned up and joined our flock, arrived with nine chicks. We weren't exactly overjoyed, because as much as we love having chicks we need to stop our flock growing out of control and we knew that half those chicks would be roosters.

But we nurtured them and eventually Top Knot buggered off and left them in their cage for us to look after. Once they were big enough to get into the trees we let them go free-range but not before killing the roosters. I now have a very good idea of how roosters look at about six weeks old and hide in the house while Paul finishes them off.

Every year we decide that we'll give the new hens away to someone, but then we fall in love with them and keep them, which is why we have 24 chickens.

Wild roosters

Roosters divide people. Most people dislike their loud crowing, sometimes as early as 2 a.m. and sometimes as late as 11 p.m. when there is a full moon. Some say they are vicious, nasty things who will attack their owners and bite the hand that feeds them.

But some people, like myself, cannot get enough of them. My second rooster, Rusty (named after his predecessor, who featured in my book *A Natural Year*), and his son Beau were beautiful specimens, covered in glossy black, orange and white feathers and standing tall and proud. Not only that, but they were also essential for breeding. They spent much of their day jumping on my hens and thereby fertilising their eggs. Someone once told me that eating fertilised eggs is much better for you than unfertilised because they are 'a living entity'. I try not to think too much about that.

Both roosters loved nothing better than finding food for their hens and calling them over. They would dig and scratch until they found some worms, then make a peculiar sort of 'gobble, gobble' sound to summon the hens, standing back while their hens had a feed.

If I offer them treats they will take them then throw them on the ground in front of the hens rather than eat them themselves. At first I thought this was the ultimate in gentlemanly acts, until I realised that soon after the hen had started eating the treats, they were treated to a rooster mounting them from behind. They're clever, my roosters.

They are also heroes. One evening I was sitting on the steps of the hen house watching my flock have their dinner. There are four social tiers among the hens, with the oldest being the boss hens, down to the youngest being constantly bossed. I always count the little chicks to make sure none of them has disappeared during the day. In the country they can often be picked up by the hawks who fly over looking for prey.

As I was absorbed in this cosy scene the whole flock suddenly disappeared. There was no noise or warning, they just all faded silently into the bushes in a matter of seconds. It was as if someone had taken a blanket and just swept them all to one side.

I had never seen them do this before and peered into the trees to see what was going on. The adult hens were shielding the babies and they were all standing perfectly still as though they were playing that game 'Freeze!' we all played as kids.

Hens don't often stand still, so it must have been a huge effort for them. Then I noticed that the strict social hierarchy had been abandoned. Top hens were standing side by side with mid-ranked hens who were standing next to lower-class hens.

What could cause such unusual cooperation, I wondered? I looked to the sky, and there it was. A huge hawk cruising overhead in a casual manner, although I could sense he was poised to attack.

Only then did I notice that the two roosters, Beau and Rusty, had not been swept away in the tide of hens. They were standing out in the open, heads to one side, staring at the hawk. Their legs were wide, their feathers were puffed out and they were strutting.

'Come on and have a go,' they seemed to be saying. 'Bring it on!'

My roosters had turned into warriors, prepared for battle, marching up and down the driveway, ready to take on the hawk.

'You little beauties,' I said as I watched them protect their flock.

It was all over in five minutes and the hens were soon back to feeding, bullying and bickering, and most of all the little chicks were safe.

I rushed back to the house and brought back treats. Dried mealworms and fresh corn on the cob were offered to Rusty and Beau, and for once they both had a good feed before offering it to the flock. I guess in cases of immense heroism, food comes before sex.

Wild death

Beau and Rusty lived harmoniously together for years — I have since realised that this is not usual. Most roosters don't like having another hanging around but Rusty accepted his son immediately. I never saw them have a bad word or fight and they protected the flock as a team.

That was until one morning when I went to feed the hens and noticed that Rusty was not himself. He was barely moving and covered in blood. At first I thought a stoat or wild cat had attacked him and was just leaning in for a closer look when out of the blue came Beau at full run to attack him. Rusty somehow found some energy and took off with Beau in pursuit. By the time I caught up with them, Beau was using the spurs on his legs to stab his father repeatedly. I managed to kick him off and there was Rusty, covered in blood and close to death.

It was such a shock to see so much violence take place between two animals I thought were friends.

Paul was working in town and Dad was away in his caravan so it was up to me to sort this out. I lifted Rusty into a cardboard box lined with hay and set him up by the fire. Most chickens will recover well from shock or sickness if you pop them in a box by the fire for the night. I often do this if one of my hens is having a hard moult, which means they lose most of their feathers and get very cold. It helps keep them warm and ready to face the day.

I went to bed, sure that in the morning I would peer into that box and find Rusty dead. At 5 a.m. he started crowing. Old habits die hard.

When I looked in, he was still very, very sick and lifeless.

I needed to put him out of his misery, but I've never killed a chicken in my life. I rang a friend, who said she could find someone to do it and they would probably make a meal of him too as he was a big bird. I was fine with this as it meant my rooster didn't go to waste.

Later she told me that he was covered in puncture wounds when they plucked him for the pot, so I was right to kill him when I did.

Beau then began to be a bit of a shit. My favourite rooster, who had cuddled into me as a young boy and survived when his brothers didn't simply because I loved him, acted like someone had given him a shot of testosterone. He strutted, posed and bossed his flock around. He was horrible.

When we tried to introduce Tonga, one of our new roosters, to Beau, he wasn't having any of it. No wonderful companionship like he'd had with his dad, Rusty. No protecting the flock together. He would chase Tonga all day, terrifying him, and I knew that if Tonga was ever caught off guard that would be the end of him.

In the end I sent my beloved Beau off to the pot because when you get an aggressive strain in your flock, that is not good. It was clear that Tonga was Rusty's offspring because he had the same red colouring as his dad, while Beau had beautiful dark plumage.

It needed to happen.

Tonga couldn't quite believe his luck when Beau disappeared and he quickly stepped into the role of top rooster. I'm pleased to say that he's a softy like his dad, as I never, ever want to see that kind of violence on my property again.

Epilogue

While this book was being edited, I had an email from a journalist wanting to talk about women my age having a midlife crisis and 'how we were raised to believe we could have it all, and yet many of us are now exhausted and disappointed'.

I felt like emailing back 'Mate, I've just written The Book on that topic.'

Some of my friends, on hearing I had written this book, seemed surprised that I'd managed to write a third book on natural living. 'What, another one?' they said. Which is similar to the reaction some of my friends had each time I announced I was pregnant . . . again.

But writing a book is a lot like being pregnant, to be honest. You set off full of hopes and dreams, feel nauseous a lot, then settle into what you think is a lovely creative time during your second trimester. During the third trimester you wallow and wail with the enormity of it all.

This book was exactly like that. I wanted to share some good stuff with you. Ocean swimming, making amazing compost, exiting social media, breathing well and eating more fibre. But I also wanted to keep talking about living a natural life full of diversity, and in particular in these times, keeping your mental health safe and cared for, as well as looking after your friends and family and their mental health.

I wrote about things that were helping me, in the hope that they would help you too. I thought there might be something in these pages that would spark your interest or encourage you to do something differently to help you live a more natural life.

I did do that interview with the journalist. It made me realise that there's a perception out there that I have it all: a life in the country, freelance work, swimming every day, hens, cats, dogs and a great husband and father to love and be loved by.

I'm grateful for all of that but believe me, I'm still working on getting it right and I make lots of mistakes. I've only recently worked out how to spend a few hours reading a book in the sun without feeling guilty about it. I've only just learned how to slow down to a pace that is more achievable. I'm still learning how to pull back from over-parenting my adult children, to make sure I prioritise sleep and to keep eating the foods my body likes and needs to be healthy.

So it's never really finished, this natural life. It's an ongoing process, but it's one we can all share and help each other with. I hope the ideas in this book will help you a little in your search for a more natural life too.

Acknowledgements

I would like to thank all the wonderful people I interviewed originally for *Thrive* magazine who generously allowed me to use their quotes again. There were a lot of emails sent out and you all got back to me, so many thanks for that.

I would also like to thank all the authors who wrote the amazing books that I read as research. Books like yours really are changing the world.

On that, big thanks to my family and friends who had to listen to me every time I finished a book and insisted on telling them all about my latest findings in the world of health and natural living. They all got really good at nodding and saying 'How interesting' at the right times.

Thanks to Allen & Unwin, who have been kind enough to publish five of my books now. My publisher, Jenny Hellen, persuaded me to write the first book in my natural series, *The Natural Home*, and she has been such a supportive and gentle hand since then. Leanne McGregor has the horrible job of wrangling the production of my books and does it with patience and understanding. Tracey Wogan edited my second book, *Bitch & Famous*, 14 years ago, and was kind enough to return to one of my manuscripts. And of course thanks to publicist Abba Renshaw, who always works wonders making sure people know when my books are out there to buy.

A grateful thank you to designer Kate Barraclough, who has made all three of my natural books beautiful.

Recommended podcasts

How to Fail with Elizabeth Day
Great interviews with well-known people who describe three of their failures. I highly recommend the episodes featuring Derren Brown, Graham Norton, Marian Keyes and Dr Nicole LePera.

Sugar Calling
Cheryl Strayed is an advice columnist in *The New York Times*. Here she rings up well-known writers for a chat.

Courage and Spice
Sas Petherick is a Kiwi living in England who is a coach specialising in self-doubt. Worth a dip occasionally.

Just One Thing with Michael Mosley
Dr Michael Mosley spends just 15 minutes telling you about one thing you can do to be healthier. His dark chocolate episode is particularly inspiring.

Conversations
Nothing to do with self-help but all about nice long-form interviews with interesting people. Great for a long car trip. Produced by the ABC in Australia.

The Inquiry
Produced by the BBC World Service, these are 25-minute documentaries featuring four experts on issues of the day. Great if you're confused about something like whether our phones are spying on us or if we can make the super-rich pay more tax.

WTF with Marc Maron

Occasionally Marc can be quite self-help-oriented, particularly when he's talking about himself, which he does a lot. But mainly he does great interviews with interesting people. Ignore his self-indulgent guitar solo at the end; it's a bit like having to listen to your first boyfriend play 'Stairway to Heaven' on his new guitar.

River Café Table 4

Ruth Rogers, chef and owner of the infamous River Café, interviews some of her regular customers. Fabulous.

Up To Speed with Te Reo Māori

Stacey and Scotty Morrison are at the forefront of easing Aotearoa into more use of our national language. This is a great start. I love it.

Recommended reading

Here are some of the authors and books I've referred to throughout, in case you'd like to delve into any of the topics in more detail.

Joanna Blythman, *What to Eat: Food that's good for your health, pocket and plate*, Fourth Estate, United Kingdom, 2013

Bill Bryson, *The Body: A guide for occupants*, Penguin, United Kingdom, 2019

Elizabeth Day, *How To Fail: What I've learned from things going wrong*, Fourth Estate, United Kingdom, 2020

Bridget Elworthy and Henrietta Courtauld, *The Land Gardeners: Cut flowers*, Thames & Hudson, Australia, 2020

Dave Goulson, *Silent Earth: Averting the insect apocalypse*, Jonathan Cape, United Kingdom, 2021

Johann Hari, *Lost Connections: Why you're depressed and how to find hope*, Bloomsbury Publishing, United Kingdom, 2019

John Harris, *The Natural Gardener: A lifetime of gardening by the phases of the moon*, John Blake Publishing, United Kingdom, 2020

Johanna Knox, *The Forager's Treasury: The essential guide to finding and using wild plants in Aotearoa*, Allen & Unwin, New Zealand, 2021

Nicole LePera, *How to Do the Work: Recognise your patterns, heal from your past + create your self*, Orion Spring, United Kingdom, 2021

Robert H Lustig, *Metabolical: The truth about processed food and how it poisons people and the planet*, Yellow Kite, United Kingdom, 2021

Nicole Masters, *For the Love of Soil: Strategies to regenerate our food production system*, Integrity Soils, New Zealand, 2019

James Nestor, *Breath: The new science of a lost art*, Penguin Life, United Kingdom, 2021

Jenny Odell, *How to Do Nothing: Resisting the attention economy*, Black Inc, Australia, 2019

Michael Pollan, *Cooked: A natural history of transformation*, The Penguin Press, United States, 2013

Michael Pollan, *Food Rules: An eater's manual*, Penguin Books, United Kingdom, 2010

Michael Pollan, *How to Change Your Mind: The new science of psychedelics*, Penguin Books, United Kingdom, 2019

Michael Pollan, *The Omnivore's Dilemma: The search for a perfect meal in a fast-food world*, Bloomsbury Publishing, United Kingdom, 2011

Merlin Sheldrake, *Entangled Life: How fungi make our worlds, change our minds and shape our futures*, Random House, United States, 2020

Suzanne Simard, *Finding the Mother Tree: Uncovering the wisdom and intelligence of the forest*, Allen Lane, United Kingdom, 2021

Tim Spector, *Spoon-Fed: Why almost everything we've been told about food is wrong*, Jonathan Cape, United Kingdom, 2020

Tim Spector, *The Diet Myth: The real science behind what we eat*, Weidenfeld & Nicholson, United Kingdom, 2016

Sue Stuart-Smith, *The Well-Gardened Mind: Rediscovering nature in the modern world*, William Collins, United Kingdom, 2021

Isabella Tree, *Wilding: The return to nature of a British farm*, Picador, United Kingdom, 2019

Chris Voss, *Never Split the Difference: Negotiating as if your life depended on it*, Random House, United Kingdom, 2017

Kate Wall, *Working with Weeds: A practical guide to understanding, managing and using weeds*, Katrina Wall, United States, 2019

Rosamund Young, *The Secret Life of Cows*, Faber & Faber, United Kingdom, 2017

PRICE 2.-   TRIED RECIPES   SIXTH EDITION

DOMESTIC ECONOMY   Ada Clley

NATIVE *Birds* OF NEW ZEALAND   REED

Recipe index

First published in 2022

Some of the material in this book has been published in different versions in *Thrive* magazine. The publisher would like to thank School Road Publishing for their assistance.

Allen & Unwin
Level 2, 10 College Hill, Freemans Bay
Auckland 1011, New Zealand
Phone: (64 9) 377 3800
Email: auckland@allenandunwin.com
Web: www.allenandunwin.co.nz

83 Alexander Street
Crows Nest NSW 2065, Australia
Phone: (61 2) 8425 0100

A catalogue record for this book is available from the National Library of New Zealand.

ISBN 978 1 98854 770 1

Design by Kate Barraclough
Set in Adobe Caslon Pro
Printed by C&C Offset Printing Co., Ltd, China

10 9 8 7 6 5 4 3 2 1